MW00935130

DIVINE HEALING

Powerful Stories of Transformation With Higher Selves and Beings of Light

CAROL ANNE HALSTEAD et al

One Printers Way
Altona, MB R0G 0B0
Canada

www.friesenpress.com

First Edition — 2023

ISBN
978-1-03-918864-8 (Hardcover)
978-1-03-918863-1 (Paperback)
978-1-03-918865-5 (eBook)

1. BODY, MIND & SPIRIT, HEALING

Distributed to the trade by The Ingram Book Company

Table of Contents

This book is dedicated to our Higher Selves, the Ascended Masters,
Archangels, Guides and all Beings of Light
who work through us to help others heal

Preface

Welcome to a book that could change your life. If you are looking for unconventional ways to assist you on your healing path and want to work with exceptional healers, this book is for you. We are ten healers worldwide who share intimate stories of challenging life circumstances, our successful efforts to overcome these challenges, and the development of our extraordinary gifts, knowledge, and healing practices. We all embody our Higher Selves.

Our Higher Selves work through us to create healing for others.

Our Higher Selves want to show the world how they can work through us (their lower selves) to bring divine truth, wisdom, and healing to others. The stories in this book are about transformation and often miraculous healing for both humans and animals. They are meant to offer hope to people seeking healing, guidance, or clarity. You will read about change, transformation, and positive, uplifting outcomes that have brought happiness, joy, and peace to those receiving the healings. There is healing energy infused in the words in this book. This is the energy of joy, love, peace, and hope.

There are stories in this book that you may relate to because of an experience you had in your own life. You may even share one or more of the stories with a friend who has gone through something similar.

Our Higher Selves want to bring a message of hope to the world in these challenging times by bringing these stories of extraordinary healing together in a book format.

This book is a gift of love from our Higher Selves to you.

The Higher Self

The Higher Self is a vast, multidimensional being. There is one for each soul. Each one is unique. Their purpose is to help our souls ascend, and in turn ascend themselves. They do this by creating life after life for us to experience. They design each human life with the capacity to realize its true nature. This is the awakening that is happening now on the planet. This has happened to each of us. We are all on a journey of Ascension, and now we can work with our Higher Selves directly in service as healers. Most of the healers in this book have their Higher Selves fully embodied in their "Holy Hearts." The rest are on their way. This is the result of years of Ascension work.

You can read about the Higher Self at: www.alphaimagiing.co.nz

The Healers

There was an unexpected pivot point for each of us in our lives, which caused us all to shift in a different direction. You will read about our stories of grief, loss, and disempowerment; from stability to instability and then finding a new base; and of paradigm shifts. We describe the sometimes deeply challenging and lonely journey to wholeness. We describe the healing methods we have been guided to develop and use with our clients. We relate many joyful and uplifting stories of successful healings. But there is so much more to our work than applying a certain technique. The fact that our Higher Selves are working through us to benefit the client is exceptional. Each healer has a high spiritual vibration due to our steady Ascension work, and every client benefits greatly from the high resonance of the healer. The healers here all work directly with not just their Higher Self, but they also work with other Ascended Masters, angels and Archangels, other Beings of Light and Guides. Each one provides unique services. It is all about helping people in a variety of ways. We offer a holistic healing model. It is based on Love. We are the conduits for the vast healing energies of our Higher Selves and these loving Beings of Light. I highly recommend that you open the website, www.ascendinginitiates.com and look at the initiates page to connect with us through our photos.

The Chapters

There are ten chapters in this book, each one written by an individual healer. The ten healers are from Canada, the USA, Australia, Brunei, and the UK. We describe how we became healers, our Ascension paths, and stories of successful healings that will inspire you.

The spelling, grammar and punctuation styles used in each chapter reflect the conventions of the region where the healer resides.

The chapters have been energetically laid out for the best reading and receiving information flow. In these chapters, we:

- relate stories of overcoming difficult personal challenges.
- describe our processes of personal healing and self-discovery.
- describe our journeys of awakening and remembering our gifts and talents.
- tell our Ascension stories.
- describe our unique healing abilities, gifts, and strategies.
- show how we help others who have struggled in some aspect of their lives.
- bring a positive, inspiring message of joy and hope.

The Ascended Masters

The "new" Masters are the ones who have become fully embodied in living, breathing human beings who are residing on the planet at this time. They are known to us by their colors that are not visible to "the naked eye" but are very beautiful, shining, brilliant colors that represent their rays and sphere of influence. These are visible to those "with sight to see," the clairvoyants with this gift of inner vision. These new Masters are our Higher Selves and show themselves to us individually in unique garb and physical appearance. Each new Master has a specific area of expertise and can be called upon directly for help. You will read about our Higher Selves in each of the chapters.

You may have heard about the famous Ascended Masters who lived on Earth in ancient times. They are well-known Ascended Masters, and many books, articles, and websites have plenty of information about who they are, what they look like, and how they are helping humanity now. Some of the most famous Ascended Masters are Jesus, Mother Mary, Mary Magdalene, Hilarion, St Germain, John the Baptist, Kuan Yin, Melchizedek, and Serapis Bey, and there are countless others. These and many other Masters have chosen to help humanity with their Ascension. (There are also many, many Masters who are working in other areas, not with humanity at this time.)

The Shift

There is an extraordinary shift taking place on the planet. People on Earth are waking up slowly. They are recognizing truth versus falsehood and are no longer willing to accept deceit or attempts to control their lives. This creates change within our institutions because what no longer works must adapt. There is also more evidence of a growing desire to connect with a higher purpose as the recognition dawns that life is so much more.

The truth is we enter this life with a body/mind/soul, a set of circumstances and a soul path. According to astrology, the point at which we take our first breath determines our precise traits and personality. But we come in blind. We don't remember where we came from or why we are here. We also have a certain karmic load accumulated from our prior lives. The principle of reincarnation is at play until we can "wake up" to our divine purpose on Earth. Once we wake up, we can work to clear our karmic history from our chakras, and in doing so we raise our spiritual vibration. Once we have cleared our karma, we no longer reincarnate. We have started the journey to reconnect to our Source. The long journey can be said to be a journey "home." We have all lived so many lives where we have not understood this. In these times, momentum is gathering for sharing and understanding the idea of Ascension as the big task of our lives. Ascension is our way off the cycle of rebirth. It is accomplished through clearing our chakras of the karmic load we have incarnated with each lifetime. It is a very personal and sometimes challenging journey as we face our own shadow and bring it to the Light.

This is the human story. Why is it so hard to remember our divine nature? One reason is that Earth is an experiment with free will. It may be hard to accept that we are loved unconditionally by a Creator when we look at our world. We see crime, greed, poverty, death, loss, disease, climate crisis, war, and inhumane acts, even amidst the good that is also being accomplished here. Once someone has awoken, they can see a much broader picture. They can see that their circumstances have been pre-designed to wake them up out of their slumber. It is a difficult task, but we have many helpers from the spiritual world all around us waiting to be invited in to help. God has blessed our world with angels and Archangels who, without their own free will, are fully available and on call to help. There are also the Ascended Masters, Cosmic Masters, Elohim, and other Beings of Light. There are so many planetary and cosmic beings of light guiding us at this time, it is beyond comprehension. "Wake up, wake up, wake up!" they say. "We are here to help. Call on us!"

We won't ever know the whole origin-and-purpose story. But once we understand and act on the Ascension story, our lives will move forward in ways beyond our understanding.

Ascension

Ascension is the journey from our darkness into light. Each of us has found a spiritual path that led to the work of clearing all our accumulated karma created over many lifetimes on Earth. We will no longer reincarnate on this Earth school. Our lessons have all been learned. We do not need to return to Earth in yet another lifetime where we are veiled from the truth of our being. Everyone in this book has accomplished this. The earthly journey is about experiencing separation from our Creator through duality and finding a path to reunification through Love. We have had to go through thousands of lives to get to the point of being able to clear our karma. This work also causes a rise in our spiritual vibration, allowing us to gradually embody the Higher Self.

There are defined levels of spiritual growth called initiations. While there are many initiation paths, the healers in this book have followed one that comes directly from the Ascended Masters through a sacred portal they have created through Verna Maruata and Waireti Nylah in New Zealand. Verna and Waireti have been taught by a group of Ascended Masters who have brought their wisdom, healings, and products through this sacred portal. These Ascended Masters are here to help humanity with our Ascension. They have brought a new clear, precise, and quick system. It can be accomplished within a few years. Whereas it took many years and multiple lives to create small shifts in our karma and vibration, now anyone can achieve freedom from the cycle of reincarnation in this one lifetime. Each of us in this book describes our personal Ascension journey.

There are well-defined steps to each level. There is no hall pass or instant enlightenment. Staying on track and committing fully to this process is important to walking this path. The quiet reward is the deep and loving connection that develops with your Higher Self once you pass the sixth initiation. The Higher Self becomes your best resource, teacher, and guide. These steps come slowly and happen only when we are ready. We need to become cleaner vessels first. Hence clearing our karma is the first step. Our karma is 100 percent cleared once we pass the fifth initiation. After passing the sixth initiation, our Higher Self anchors into our Holy Heart. We first learn how to find our Sacred Heart and then the Holy Heart within it. The concept of the Sacred Heart is well-known within some religions. It holds God's Will, Love, and Wisdom within its trifold flame. It is depicted on statues of Jesus in Catholic Churches around the world.

Most of the healers in this book have passed the seventh initiation or are close to passing it now. Our Higher Selves are 100 percent embodied when we pass the seventh initiation. At this point, our Higher Selves are known as the new Masters.

Rays

There are eight rays of light which are the energy manifestations of the attributes of God. Each ray has unique colors, purposes, and alignment with Ascended Masters, Elohim, Cosmic Masters, and Archangels. Each of the healers here is on a specific ray. We also have sub-rays. My Higher Self is on the fifth Ray of knowledge, healing, and truth, and hence so am I. This has always made sense to me as my need to learn, discover, and teach has been relentless. My Higher Self is now fully embodied in my Holy Heart, and this loving relationship continues to grow. My Higher Self has plans which he reveals over time. For instance, I have known for a while that a second book (the first is called *Modern Ascension*) was to be written, but this time it would be about healers who work with their Higher Selves, Ascended Masters, and other Beings of Light to help others. The Higher Selves of each contributor to this book are working together to bring this book into being. They want to spread the word about the exceptional healings they offer through their lower selves; that is, the healers in this book. The fact that our Higher Selves work through us to help others is unique. The methods we use are inspired and taught to us by them. We serve with humility, gratitude, and devotion to our beloved Higher Selves.

An Invitation

If you would like to connect with one of the many healers in this book, please contact any of us for more information. We can answer your questions so you can decide if there is a fit.

You may feel that your problems are too large and chronic to recover. You may have tried everything and yet remain debilitated in some ways. Or conversely, you may think that because some of the healings you read about are so significant, your issues are too small to be addressed by any of the healers here. None of that is true.

You are important. Your life is important. You deserve to be happy and healthy.

Many of the healers here can work remotely with you no matter where you live. We welcome the opportunity to provide our healing services to help you in your life. We do not dismiss the benefits of medical care. Our work does not replace the important work of clinical diagnosis and medical treatment. But we can work with you wherever you are in the healing process. We invite your inquiries.

The Cover

The cover of this book has the colors of each of our Higher Selves. It also has been imprinted by all the Higher Selves with their vast energy. It is powerful image.

Carol Anne Halstead

Chapter One

Healing Art Heals the Soul

by Tamara Liz Rivera Hyde

I am far from perfect, but I try my best to follow my heart's divine guidance. The heart is the keeper of my Higher Self, who is gentle, loving, and uplifting. So gentle that sometimes it escapes my attention!

-Tamara Liz

Life is always preparing us to fulfill our purpose. Pushing us to learn the lessons we cower from. Those lessons can take us closer to God and thus higher in vibration. While life can get tough, it is not solely for paying karma. It also enlightens our path and drives us forward, even when we think we are not progressing. Most of the time we have simply signed up for the experience, always with the same goal to unite with God. Then there are forces that attack us when we are not spiritually guarded. For this lifetime, I signed up for a mental health breakdown. The second one was a direct attack. However, both served me...

When my mom was pregnant with me, they told her I was stillborn. Thankfully, she looked for another opinion. She was sent to bed rest. On the morning of the day of commemoration of the Virgin of Mount Carmel in Puerto Rico, my uncle took my mom to the hospital. My dad, who worked the night shift as a forensic photographer, came home to find out my mom was not there. Before heading to the hospital, he released all the birds he collected as an offering to God. He asked Him to save me and ensure everything would be fine with my birth. I was told by Verna that my soul came in at birth. Such is life, always working out perfectly; even when it may not be perceived as such. Throughout this chapter, I will mention Verna and Waireti, who have been fundamental to my Ascension journey. I learned all about the Ascended Masters and more through their website <alphaimaging.co.nz>.

As a child, family and friends called me a free spirit. Mostly because my family expected me to behave or be a certain way, and I would never comply. To be fair, my family was excessively strict, and I have always been who I am. Free spirit was adequate, considering I had no karmic lessons in my childhood. The truth is that nowadays, the behavior I exhibited as a child would be deemed textbook ADHD. I may have always been neurodivergent, but nobody knew. They would tell me not to step in the puddle, and I was already there. I was simply too distracted to see the puddle in time. It was not because I wanted to do my will over theirs. Other times I directly challenged their outdated systems, always asking why. As my mom, a retired teacher, would lovingly say now: "You were not like other kids." To them, I was an unruly, willful child who happened to be creative. A package deal: a little rebel with artistic inclination.

Early on, people noticed I could make art without looking at anything to copy. My abuelo, who was also an artist, was particularly surprised when I reproduced a popular cartoon from memory. In fact, my mom saved one of my first drawings at age four; a nativity scene on a napkin. Art was also my coping mechanism in school. I was always doodling. Doodling and manipulating clay or a stress ball while listening to information can help process it. That detail was unavailable back then, but it still worked in my favor. While the teacher worked on her lesson, I could simultaneously listen, doodle, and be lost in my thoughts. I had a rich inner world, even if I did not verbalize it. They would say I was always in the clouds. They were right. I remember being in third grade and having a nun teach us about heaven. I never said anything, but I imagined we would not have bodies in "heaven." We would be floating, colorful consciousness. It was great to read Verna and Waireti describe how the Ascended Masters see us similarly.

I feel blessed that I can guide my beloved children through their Ascension path, even as I am still learning. On the other hand, I grew up with a lot of dogma. Having a busy mind as I did, I would sometimes argue with myself. I would self-punish to be better for God. I wanted to feel close to Him and be good enough for Him. I wanted to feel His guidance, but I cannot deny that I struggled. I could barely keep track of my prayers. I would jump to something else mid-sentence, interrupted by my wandering mind. I did not know what silence inside my head was for many years, not for a second. Even when I had my mom take me to a child psychologist at age fourteen, all I got was my debut on TV. My mom recalls how the psychologist said she identified with me; perhaps this is why she selected me for an interview she had on a local TV channel. I don't remember much from that interview, but I was nervous and did not perform how I usually would. I actually forgot about it until years later, when I briefly watched the recording on VHS and felt estranged.

That was the first time I dissociated, but I did not know. I knew that I was different. I mean, who takes their Ouija board to Catholic school or does their science fair project about life after death? I am not kidding! I am proud of my childhood self because I loved being outspoken, daring, and out of the box. What worried me was how I could shift emotions in a split second. A particular event always left me wondering. I was in a classroom with my friends in high school. They were telling jokes, and I could not control my laughter. One of the jokes quickly turned my laughter into devastated crying. I do not remember the particulars; only that it was about people with developmental disabilities. My only contact with people with developmental disabilities had been at a waterpark when I was about six years old. However, it must have been impactful. I had never met someone with a developmental disability, and there seemed to be hundreds at this point. I do not remember much about my feelings, but I continued playing. Was that reaction in high school part of an illness or a hint at a past life? I just felt scared that I could shift emotions without any conscious trigger.

I thought I had ADHD, but turns out, with my first mental health breakdown, it was more complicated. I remember how I slowly began to lose my mind. It was 2005. I was twenty-three years old. I had already finished an associate degree, and I was working retail and finishing a Bachelor's in Fine Art at a prestigious art school in Old San Juan. I was getting married three days before I was hospitalized. We had planned the wedding in three months because I wanted to move in with my boyfriend, and our families wanted us married. It was truly my dream wedding; the ceremony would be by the beach and the reception at the beach club. I was elated. I was moving to a small but glorious apartment in Old San Juan. It was perfect. Minus a few silly details, like my family did not like my fiancé. My uncle, who is like another dad to me, had announced in protest that he would not attend my wedding. I had hundreds of wedding decisions to make. I was sick with asthma, taking medications, and had stopped eating for a better dress fit. Stressor after stressor, it was not looking good for me. The next thing I knew, I was walking in the strip mall Plaza Centro. I could hear a pop song playing loudly. I looked around because they did not play music in this strip mall. I knew I was not fully there, but I managed to drive back home. The chronology of events is a little blurry, but I do remember most of it. I could not sleep, so I began to write about love. I was obsessed with my fiancé. It was not my first lifetime with him. I later learned he believed I had the episode because I did not want to marry him. Silly rabbit. There are easier ways to end a wedding. Having a psychotic episode, AKA losing your mind, would not be my first choice.

For a while, I thought I was dead and landed in purgatory. The first night I was strapped to a bed, singing church songs that I would sing with my dad. I was so thirsty I asked the male nurse to kiss me. My delusional mind thought that would help me. The nurse must have been in a worse state of mind because he did. During the day, I would walk up and down a corridor, wondering if I had killed my family in a car accident and was being punished. I felt like I was locked inside my mind. I barely spoke. At one point I was in a catatonic state, submerged in my mind. I was taken into the Milky Way and learned about love and the great mother while a strange lady I shared the room with cuddled me. I remember it was a Wednesday, about a week after being hospitalized, that my family visited. That changed everything. To begin with, now I knew I was alive. My mom asked them to lower my medicine, and soon I was putting myself back together. Not long after that, I told the psychiatrist I had an existential crisis (mind you, I knew nothing about psychology; that was a download) but that I was fine. I told him about my dreams and goals, and that I wanted to be known as an artist in my social sphere; to make it in the art world. The doctor thought I had grandiosity ideations but was surprised by my recovery. I would go on to make myself known in the art world, sell my art, and make and exhibit video art about that experience.

How do you even begin to process that experience? Or the transition back to life? In all honesty, the doctors I saw did not help. I inevitably took the familiar approach of moving forward without processing; that is, until I began to use my creative outlets to explore my experiences...

There was a period of intense pain, heartache, and self-destruction; yet at the same time I worked tirelessly toward my dreams. When you have so much in your mind, it is cumbersome to self-express adequately, but art became a way to conceptualize my experience, learn more about myself, and express what I could not otherwise.

The first time I realized the transformative power of art was when I was in tears in front of my experimental painting class, showing my artwork of what looked like a blocked sacral chakra. I did not even know what chakras were at the time. I did not comprehend how that painting was symbolically (and quite literally) speaking to me. All I knew was that I had made it while mentally processing my experience. As I spoke about it in the classroom, I realized it represented so much of my inner turmoil. I had officially purged my pain into that painting. It took me years to gain the knowledge to understand that I had energetically transferred my pain into the canvas. I did not have the words or knowledge yet, but I had felt it.

Simultaneously with this process, my inclination toward spirituality began to shift, grow, and expand. I was in the flow, even if life was not perfect. When I began working on my Bachelor's thesis, I decided to try medication to help me organize my ideas. The medicine I was prescribed stopped my racing thoughts. It was the first time I felt peace and quiet in my mind. I did not use the medicine for long; however, its effects became permanent. My thought process slowed down, and the noise stopped. I was able to see the signs in my life much more clearly. This is when I began to talk to birds. I could intuitively receive their messages as a knowing or nudge. On one occasion, the birds told me a friend should visit their family. My friend's rational mind was quick to dismiss the message. Their cousin, who I had met before, passed away days after. When I first met their cousin, I could feel immense love for him. He had severe developmental disabilities, yet his soul was there. I knew exactly when he passed. I felt it in my heart. That same year, I felt a flame in my heart for a solid three days. Much like how I feel Higher Self now. I was practicing messianic Judaism, and the symbols and downloads were huge. With blessings and synchronicity left and right, I was selling my art and creating more art linked to kabbalah and the creation myths. It was great, but I was afraid of the weight on my shoulders. As if I was supposed to complete something important. Either way, the entire process helped me shift gears—I stepped into love and understanding. Everything that happened, everyone I met, catapulted me into the person I would become.

Fast forward to 2018, and I am living in Atlanta. Life was not a cakewalk, but I managed to do as best I could. I am married and have beautiful, amazing kids. I earned a Master's degree in Art Therapy. I exhibited art as part of a collective of Hispanic artists and gave Art Therapy workshops at our local art guild. I was helping the community by volunteering to work with churches and nonprofits. I developed my own business and offered art therapy online, but since it was hard to do it alone, I went into business with others. It did not work out, rather it turned out to be toxic. I felt defeated. I had put so much work and energy into it. I tried to advocate for myself, but I felt walked over. Once again, the stressors were remarkably high, and I had recently started taking medication. A series of events elapsed, including contact with artistic images with extremely negative energy. I remember everything. I slowly but surely lost contact with reality. The treatment was horrible. They transferred me without my family's consent—they had me sign while I was out of it. For two days, my family did not know where I was. I had no clothes. I was treated very poorly—this time for completely different circumstances. That was until my husband located me and handed them my business card. After seeing my husband, I started to regain consciousness. It was hard, for so many reasons. One was that I wanted to go back to my life as me, as if another soul could shift into my body. It was bizarre. Two was that I was ashamed to have lost my mind being a therapist. I know better, but sometimes you can't help how you feel. Third was that putting your mind back together is hard work. When I told my story to begin my discharge, the therapist there was sure it was a spiritual attack. She was right. Back home, my mom and abuela had lit candles that exploded while they spiritually cleansed the house. To this day, there are things that I cannot comprehend. Per usual, I have done my own therapy with this. Both experiences resemble spiritual awakenings, albeit tainted. Mental health breakdowns, filled with fears, are not what spirituality is. This second one was extremely evil. The delusions were terrifying. I had lived without fear for years, but after that episode I lived in fear for a few weeks. As you can imagine, I took to painting...

As much as I love painting, I can safely say that I read more than I paint. I have always been thirsty for spiritual knowledge. During the weeks after the attack, I found an amazing, documented story of a living apparition of the Virgin of Mount Carmel in Puerto Rico. I painted my perception of her and the incredible story of her ten years in the body "apparition." They called her Elenita de Jesus. I know now she was not an apparition of the Virgin of Mount Carmel; she was an exceptional Ascended Master from another world. I did not know about the Ascended Masters; however, her story helped me to soon find Verna and Waireti amidst the upheaval in my life.

I had never been into politics, but I lived in Georgia, where discrimination was rampant. I could not believe so many people supported a man that acted in such harmful ways. He threw paper towels at people after Hurricane Maria in Puerto Rico. I was livid. My mom, who went for a short visit, was stuck on the island. She had been such an incredible support for me throughout my life, but especially during that 2018 summer. Even if I did not fully understand how it affected me, when I created art the symbols spoke to me and helped me understand. I missed talking to her. At least I knew that she, my uncle, and my grandma were fine. But why did so many spiritual people support this man that trampled over an entire race? I had to deep dive to understand. I learned so much. I completely shifted my views. It seemed like this man was the only one standing up against traffickers, corruption, etc. Somehow he was serving all of us. He was disrespectful to my people, yet he was right. Our island is plagued by corrupt politicians and more. They mismanaged all the money and help they received. People woke up. He stirred everyone up, and suddenly they decided to fight for something better. In 2019, Puerto Rico managed to get their governor to resign in an uproar for all the pain it had endured. I dislike things about that man, but his presence catalyzed change. I found a small Twitter community during that lonely time when I began to learn more about Ascension. You see, when I found Verna, I thought I was at level "Saint!" (Akin to Mother Teresa or any pious person.) I have been through so much—much more than what I have shared. However, I was informed I was only on my third initiation. Oh, I have changed so much since then. Ascension has transformed my life.

Before my fifth initiation, my Ascension Ray was the fourth ray. Harmony through Conflict. I had Serapis Bey, Jesus, Kuan Yin, and Pallas Athena on my team. I did not realize before how big their influence was on my life. After my team left at the fifth initiation, I noticed a change in all levels of my personality. I am still learning about myself now. That is the path on my new ray. I am on the orange Divine Feminine of the fifth ray. I have been told by Verna that it is a light peachy color. My Higher Self, who I once knew as Nesamani, is now Derruck. I believe the name might change again, so I am not holding tight. I suspect what my sub-rays might be, but Verna has told me sub-rays show a year after the seventh initiation has passed. I have just passed the seventh initiation, therefore I will have to wait a year for confirmation. During my time in the sixth initiation, I recognize I have shifted my feelings towards the fourth and first rays. Before this, I was low-key afraid of them. I needed to understand myself more and come into more self-love and self-acceptance.

With such a big imagination, I have seen my Higher Self in different ways, including in dragon form. He is fierce and unstoppable, a force to be reckoned with. He is fully embodied, and He can be felt quite strongly. If He did not show up with such strong energy, I could have missed the experience. I am thankful that I am loved by Him. He is a creator, an artist, and a warrior. Here to break barriers and shift perspectives. He is a healer who gives us downloads and healing codes. With His sword, we eradicate implants and negative codes. I am excited to create art alongside Him.

We are ongoing works of art. Our Higher Selves' creation. As such, we continue to evolve. That process can be pleasant or as unpleasant as we make it. It is our thoughts and feelings that inform our experience. The work is never finished. I continue to learn, grow, and expand. Sometimes that looks like accepting unloved parts; parts that have been criticized or shamed. Other times it looks like a deep understanding of where our patterns come from. An example of that is a recent session I had with Tammy Manzo. We healed my past life as Frida Kahlo. Some patterns I will continue to work on, while others have been taken back by the Divine. I have written about it on my blog; you can visit <tamaraliz.com/blogs/news> to read more about that.

Healing Through Love

Growing up, being criticized or failing to meet expectations influenced my healing style and personality. I always put myself in other people's shoes. I use my super empath powers to fully understand their choices. No judgments; I just imagine different scenarios. While I may be eclectic in my therapy style, to meet client needs I often practice unconditional positive regard or unconditional love...

We all have heard about the placebo effect. There's a wide range of studies with different estimates. Some say the cure rate is 50 percent. Others assert it is from 15 to 72 percent. If you are into spirituality, you know that the placebo effect is no placebo; it is the real deal. When we align our thoughts and emotions with positive beliefs, we start to witness the shifts. A less-known truth is that the healing percentage significantly increases if the practitioner also believes you can improve. I won't say "I love you" to my clients, but that does not stop me from energetically loving the Divine in them. That is the difference that I believe I always make with my clients. They can feel the love, compassion, understanding, and non-judgmental treatment they receive from me. I stay humble because we all have been there, done that, in this life or past ones. That creates a different atmosphere in my practice. Stepping into my office/studio is like being in a healing chamber. Online sessions are no different. Those who can feel energy know. I should mention, feeling energy improves with Ascension. We can call on all our gifts, even from past lives. It may be a slow process, but it is undeniably a Blessing. If you want someone to help you process your experiences and shift gears, don't hesitate to book sessions with me. As a spiritual arts therapist, I can use all spiritual tools, including art. I may suggest or mail your materials. We talk, explore, and set intentions to transform your life. To book, visit <tamaraliz.com/products/spiritual-arts-5-sessions>.

There are stories that I wish I could tell, but I did not keep in contact with these clients to ask for permission. Their information was left behind at the clinics I worked in. There are, however, two stories I can tell. One is covered by my practicum, but I will limit the details. The other is public record, outside of clinical work, but part of my nonprofit, "Espirítu Creativo" efforts.

When I began my practicum, I decided to work with many different populations. I found a behavioral company that had different centers dedicated to different populations. I learned then that one of my favorite populations to work with is "substance abuse" clients. Some are eager to do the work because it is court-ordered, but most have too much to lose and take their sessions seriously. Most are also spiritually inclined, which is my favorite subject. For the most part, I present a bubbly personality to make art. Everyone loves that. It's the fun part of the day for most clients. Other therapists and people working there would be surprised to find that many men love Art Therapy. Not just because I would put on music and have fun with them, but because we are innately wired to self-express through art. Everyone was eager to share their artwork and tell their stories. Because I am present and genuinely interested in their stories, I tune in to the right questions. In one of my sessions, I used a directive I came up with. It is called "name etymology." I always loved researching genealogy and found beautiful stories and meaning relating to our surnames. There is so much encoded in them. Many people have stories to share about how their parents picked their names and what it means to them. Not everyone knows that our names determine many of our personality traits and more. It is quite interesting. Like astrology, the numerology in our birthdays and names has a plethora of information about us.

This exercise would prove to delight people, as they get to learn about themselves in ways they have not before. On one occasion during practicum, I used this directive with a group. A man shared his curious artwork (that I have saved to this day). Per the directive instructions, he had changed the first letter of his name and transformed it into something else. We had a fishing scene, something many of the group's men were familiar with. A detail stuck out for me, and I asked him about it. Why is the hook red? This took the man back. He realized he did not do that on purpose, yet there was a reason behind it. He shared a story about his childhood that he had not acknowledged as a traumatic event until then. That realization, and telling his story, felt cathartic to him. He was happy and proud to have shared his artwork and story. One detail, one right question. This is the power behind what I do. I help people unlock part of themselves through art.

I am about to share this event which happened in 2017, in Gwinnett County, where I lived in Georgia. A Hispanic mother stabbed her husband and five children; only one daughter survived. I did not know yet how impactful this event would be for me. All I knew when I found out was that I had to help. I reached out to the pastor who married my husband and me. He had a nonprofit organization that helped the community where this devastating event happened. We quickly organized for me to see the children who were friends with this family. I wrote up paperwork that their parents signed, and soon after, I was in the community for about three weeks doing art workshops. I gave the children an opportunity to self-express and process this major event in their lives. I encountered what could be perceived as religious dogma or misconceptions about mental health. Some of the children thought the mother was possessed, because they knew her as a nice lady. I cannot attest to whether or not she was possessed, and I would not dare interfere with their perceptions. I did educate them about mental health and how she was sick, to elicit a sense of compassion. Which they all had. It was more about the immense sadness of losing their friends and having to live and play nearby the massacre. I introduced them to different play and art activities they could integrate into their lives and use as coping skills naturally. Children are resilient. I do not know about them today, but I am positive they are fulfilling their divine purpose.

A year later, shortly after my second hospitalization, this case would resurface. A young relative with disabilities, who we loved dearly, was taken from us in a mental illness episode. She had barely been out of a facility where she had met the lady who stabbed her family. With my background, I suspected what this lady's diagnosis was, which was similar to mine. It was mind-boggling to think that could have happened to me. The lady said she was offering her children to God in exchange for bringing her father back. She also mentioned she was being chased by an evil spirit. The overlap of spiritual attacks and mental illness should not be ignored. There is a lot of work and research that should be done to further understand the implications. I can tell you that during the second hospitalization, evil forces were at play when I was attacked. It was frightening to process what I went through, considering all that could have happened. My daughter, who was in a Christian preschool learning about God and the devil, told me—while I lost contact with reality—that the devil would make her die two days from then. I do not know if you could imagine losing your mind and then hearing those words. It sent me on a mental trip. I saw how the devil could be creative, bending boundaries, and I found a way to honor the Divine in that. Even evildoers have the Divine within. I soon heard my daughter say: "You are very powerful." That scared me so much, but it mobilized me. Even as I was losing my mind, I managed to keep them safe. I went downstairs and told my husband that I was going to sleep and that our daughter should sleep in her room that night. She did not like that, but I tucked her and her brother safely in their beds and went upstairs to continue my descent into delusions. After that, I felt the urge to end my life. I would never do that, but I was no longer me. Thankfully, I was unable to stop myself. I ended up driving manically to my parents' house. That is where the spaceship would pick me up. Sounds funny now, but aliens were part of my delusion. The message I want to deliver with this story is that if you have lost someone to mental illness, remember it was no longer them making that decision. The person you knew fell victim to delusions, uncontrollable lies inside their mind, and a sickness that incapacitated their choice-making. They love you, but at that time they could not love themselves. Know that they are safe on the other side and will return to learn their lessons when the time is right.

Frequency & Vibrations

We all have frequencies and vibrations that constantly change. Our emotions and thoughts can raise or lower our vibration. We may not perceive the movement in the vibration of our cells, but it is happening. On Verna and Waireti's website, <alphaimaging.co.nz>, we learn that emotions alone can affect all our bodies. I dare to extend that and say that emotions are energies we can transfer into things and even people. After all, our bodies are composed of 45 to 75 percent water and are conductors of energy. This may be why people can always feel the positive vibes I share with them, often inspiring them to achieve their goals. People always gravitate to share with me because I listen and help shift their perspectives. Much like motivational interviewing, but the vibes do not lie. The more I understand about energies, radionics, frequencies, etc., the more I know my art can serve in many ways.

I did not wake up one day and decide to create healing art. I have been ruminating about it for years. Could you imagine art that can heal physical ailments? One day I had come to say, "Why not?" I figured color therapy could be the means to achieve that, but I hesitated to act. The truth is that I underestimated myself. I didn't believe I could do that. I mean, art that can heal people is huge. Honestly, I felt my abstract expressionism was inadequate. I had the notion that healing art had to look like Yantras. Yantras have been used in India to impart healing energy to be harnessed in life. It consists of geometric shapes and symbols that contain the energy of a planet or deity. Turns out I was just blocking myself...

I remember it was 2021. I took a free art business challenge online. We had to decide what we envision doing. I had forgotten about all the times I pondered these healing art ideas and suddenly felt illuminated. This is what I want to do with my Higher Self! I began to practice but wasn't sure how to proceed. I was in the shower when a name popped into my consciousness. "Joy." I suddenly knew I had to make my first Higher Self portal for her. I sat down with my own little ritual and began to create. My ascendant is Leo. I appear confident, but I'm often riddled with fears; therefore I couldn't bring myself to directly contact this initiate. Would she like my painting? What would she think about me just sitting down and painting her HS? Would she be upset or happy? I decided to test the waters. I posted the painting online and waited to see if she would interact, and she did! I then reached out and told her this was her HS painting. To my surprise, not only did she love it, but she had also actually purchased other Higher Self paintings. She told me she can feel energy and would test how the portal worked for her. It was a perfect match. It felt like I was destined to make this work, and I was not wrong...

Joy Vottus blogged about that experience on her website. This excerpt is her first impression of the artwork:

> "When I saw the painting, I recognized it's my Higher Self's energy—the purple and gold colors are the sixth Ray elements. My Higher Self also has some blue color in His energy signature. In the center, there is a diamond-shaped frame in a brownish color. It looks like the initial "V" for Vottus in

> the bottom part; on the top of the diamond shape are "six" curves; another synchronicity of the sixth ray. I had never mentioned anything about my Higher Self to Tamara before. She told me it's her recent work guided by her Higher Self. After conversing with her, I realized it's our Higher Self connections to produce this energy drawing through her talents. Thank you for making this happen!"

She continued:

> "This is my Higher Self's fifth Dimension energy portal, a gateway to His energy field, to other dimensions of His existence. It's connected to my Holy Heart and the eighth chakra; I could connect to this portal for healing and receiving guidance from my Higher Self. This is a sacred space for me and my Higher Self. When connected to the portal, I went into my Higher Self's energy field instantly, and there are no words to describe His powerful and loving energy. I could feel strong energy on the top of my head, as no seven-chakra system is running after I passed the fifth initiation; it felt like it was in the ex-crown chakra area."

I understood the artwork not only works energetically, but the symbols and colors that show up bring valuable insights. It can help confirm that the painting relates to the individual. Some people report that it aided them in confirming their ray colors too. I was just elated to be able to create these artworks, but my confidence would waver. I began to research different ways to prove that I was being ethical. I did not want to offer services or claim that I could do things if I was not ready yet. Fast forward after a few months of hiatus. It is now May 2022. Verna had left our Ascension group but sent a message through her assistant, Tara Jolly. The Masters were concerned about something, undisclosed to us, and asked for a Torus with the sixth and seventh initiates. Concerned sounded like worry to me; therefore I worried. I always prefer transparency, but sometimes we are not told to allow the lesson to arrive naturally. I could not help but ask myself why the Masters would express this. If everything is always happening for us, why did it require intervention? Many questions were left unanswered at that time; however we would soon find out. In preparation for the Torus, we were assigned an Ascended Master to work with. I was told to work with Mother Mary. My relationship with Mother Mary goes beyond what I could express, but working with her during that Torus renewed my self-faith. She presented me with the Flame of Trust, encouraging me to trust myself and my abilities.

Self-doubt and the inner critic are no strangers to me. I have learned to re-frame and use all the tools to get past them, but sometimes they can do a number on me. This time around, they showed up because I really want to embody integrity when I offer my services. That is a good thing. I wanted proof, evidence! Even though I have been told this is what I am meant to do and received great feedback about the art healing properties, I wanted more. The problem was that all that self-doubt got in the way. The Flame of Trust that Mother Mary introduced me to ignited me, and that same week I was asked for another painting. This time around, I did not make excuses and accepted. I knew it was meant to be. I shared this story on the <ascendinginitiates.com> website. You can learn more about it there. Long story short; I created a portal for the Twin Flame Monad and began a series of paintings about the Flame of Trust.

For me, the journey is truly about to commence. Every day I work with my Higher Self. I believe in us and the work we have embarked on. Other initiates have told us that our paintings will form pillars of light worldwide. It is all beyond what I could imagine. The ball is rolling, I am creating healing paintings. I have received grants to create more of them and provide workshops for people to learn more about using art as a spiritual tool. The road ahead is bright and exciting. I just need to maintain the joy, the inspiration, and the drive to continue knowing and serving my Higher Self.

Ahead you may enjoy the exercise I developed and mentioned in the chapter. There is healing in expressing our stories and much more when we share them. I will happily welcome you to a group where you can safely share your artwork and stories. You may sign up for private sessions, purchase my paintings, or order your own healing portal by visiting <www.tamaraliz.com> to learn more.

Name Etymology

This exercise promotes self-reflection in the process of introspection and creative flow. It is an amenable directive that guides self-discovery, new insights, and spiritual growth.

> *Materials:*
>
> Paper (if possible, no lines).
>
> If you do not have painting art materials, use colored pencils or a #2 pencil.
>
> *Instructions:*
>
> As big as you can, write the first letter of your name on a piece of paper. Look at the page and turn it around several times, pondering what you could transform this letter into. Let yourself draw a scene around it, incorporating this letter into your creation. Do not think too much; just feel the colors you want to use and the ideas that pop into your

> head. Please do not look up pictures for inspiration; you have everything you need within you. It does not have to look perfect; it is all about allowing the spirit to move within you. Ideas will flow to you, even if you do not know how to execute them. Try it. If your inner critic shows up to say hello, kindly remind it that it is all about enjoying the process and the story that unfolds through your hands.

Once you have completed your artwork, notice any symbols, colors, or shapes that have shown up. List them on a separate page. Try to write a short story about it; up to three sentences will suffice. Look up the etymology of your name or check the website <kabalarians.com> to search their name database. If possible, ask your family why they chose your name. You may share your artwork and insights with me on the Facebook group, 'Art That Transforms You' or send it to me at: becreative@tamaraliz.com

Tamara Liz Rivera Hyde, USA

Website: www.tamaraliz.com

Website: www.espiritucreativo.org

Facebook: Facebook.com/TamaraLiz

YouTube: @tamaraliz

Ascend: @5thraymaster

Instagram: @tamaraliz.art

TikTok: @tamaralizart

Chapter Two

Energetic Blockages in the Chakras Affect Both Humans and Animals

by Hayatti Rahgeni

By treating the chakras, the patient will be healed.

-Master Choa Kok Sui

My Past and How I Became a Healer: Transforming From a Victim to a Wounded Healer

I experienced a traumatic childhood and became depressed and angry in my early adulthood, but I overcame my traumatic past through self-development, energy healing, and Ascension.

My father divorced my mother when I was nine years old. More than a year later, I was raped and then sexually abused. I knew what happened was wrong, but I did not dare to tell anyone. As life progressed, no matter how much I wanted to put my past behind me, it followed me everywhere. I could not seem to escape the trauma caused by the rape and sexual abuse. As I became a young teenager, I honestly thought that prostitution was my only option. I did not care about studying or changing the direction of where I was heading. At that age, I did not know any better, and I did not know there was a way out. I thought I was stuck forever. Thankfully, I was at home pondering my future when I heard a voice in my head that said, "It doesn't have to be that way." That voice opened up my mind. I thought if there was truly another way, then let's go for it. I decided to trust that voice. My heart felt lighter because I realized that there was a way out. I finally saw that I had a bright future ahead of me. A future where I did not end up in prostitution. Since then, my attitude changed, and I started to focus and invest my energy in my studies. I am happy to share that I graduated with a degree in Science Education when I was twenty-four years old.

By the time I was twenty-five years old, I was married. My husband and I had no children, and we still have none. A few years after being married with no children, I struggled mentally because I could not cope with people's expectations. People expected me to have gotten pregnant and had children already. Eventually I became severely depressed and even suicidal. My mental illness was worsened by the childhood trauma combined with the unresolved grief and loss from my mother's unexpected death. This went on for years. I suffered for a long time until I realized I needed help. That prompted me to look for ways to help myself. My online search serendipitously led me to a world of energy healing. Initially, I did not know what it was, but I was willing to try it. While listening to an energy healer perform her healing on a telesummit, I felt something shift within me. I did not know what exactly, but I felt different. I have become a believer since then.

A year later, I came across an opportunity to learn an energy healing modality. I took the class because I wanted to learn how to heal myself. In the class, I was pleasantly surprised to discover that energy healing was effortless for me. I unlocked my first psychic ability during the class. I was able to feel energy as if it was a tangible thing. I felt like I was meant to do energy healing. After months of practice on myself, my friends, and my family, I became confident in my ability as a healer. I realized that I could help other people by offering healing. I was motivated to help people, so I started a healing business. I began working with people and accidentally unlocked another psychic ability while healing a child. It was during this healing session that it occurred to me that I was able to access the child's suppressed emotion and subsequently released it. After I was done with the healing session, I realized that I could feel which chakras have blockages and what emotions were causing the blockages. I could also feel suppressed emotions, and I could help release them. I was very excited about this psychic ability. That was the moment it became clear to me that clearing emotional blockages in the chakras is my specialty. The more I worked with people, the more I could hone my gifts, and I unlocked more psychic abilities along the way.

As a healer who wanted to heal other people, I quickly became aware that for me to support others, I needed to heal, and I worked on myself consistently. I made a commitment to heal myself, and I was adamant about healing my trauma. As much as I did countless energy healings to heal myself, I felt I did not progress as much as I should have. That was when I started to have sessions with other energy healers, and I also had a life coach. I meditated, I journaled, and I did a lot of self-reflection. Despite what I did, the trauma was still there, and my life hadn't changed much. Then one day, it finally occurred to me that nothing had changed because I was still making the same old choices. I did not want to face the trauma and would rather work on something else. I had put off healing that trauma for more than two decades. I have learned from workshops, seminars, and coaching that to create change for myself, I must start making positive and empowering choices. I then decided that enough was enough, and I chose to let go of being a victim. My journey to healing my trauma began, and more than five years later, the trauma no longer triggers me. I am at peace with what happened. Having said that, the trauma still left scars, but I take comfort in knowing that it stays in the past and it does not dictate my future.

My Ascension Journey: From Ascension to Higher Self

In late 2014, I stumbled upon the Alpha Imaging website while looking for information about Goddess Isis. The website also has information about Ascension. I did not know much about Ascension back then. When I read the information on the website, it felt like I was reading a foreign language. However, I kept returning to the website and read the information repeatedly for years.

Four years later, I finally understood what Ascension was. I had a big decision to make. Do I want to ascend? And am I willing to walk down that path? After pondering for weeks whether I should ascend or not, I saw how Ascension was very relevant to me. I felt it was long overdue. Therefore I made up my mind and chose to ascend. My Ascension journey began in late 2018, and in 2021, I passed the sixth initiation.

About a year after I passed the sixth initiation, I came across an opportunity to heal two dogs. I had never done energy healing for animals before. Nevertheless I gave it a try, and I surrendered the healing process to my Higher Self. After I was done, I was surprised that doing energy healing on animals is not that different from humans. My first energy healing session with a dog taught me so much about how unresolved emotions in humans can affect their pets. It also opened my eyes to how energy healing can help animals restore their confidence, regain their physical strength, increase their vitality, and accelerate their recovery, just like in humans. Since then, I have dedicated my energy to healing countless animals, both pets and strays.

It has been almost two years since I passed the sixth initiation. I am now close to the seventh initiation. I learn more and more about my Higher Self as I go through life and Ascension. My Higher Self's name is Yestred. He is on the third ray, the pink ray of unconditional love. His ray color is light pink. He is a warrior of light. He revealed himself as an African regal man. He is tall and thin and has an air of authority about him. He is a very serious man. He does not shy away from deep trauma. If you can feel his energy, you will feel that his energy is tough and sturdy, so one can lean on him. A few of his abilities I have discovered is that he can clear entities attached to humans and animals. He also can clear very old energy that we carry or inherit from our ancestors, either from our mother's or father's side. He is here to assist with self-love and to support those who desire to heal, empower, and transform themselves. We work as a team to create deep inner transformation for our human and animal clients.

Cassie and Weena's Healing Stories

A client, Ryan, has two older dogs called Cassie and Weena. Cassie had seizures, while Weena had vaginal bleeding. Both dogs had received three healings each. During the course of their healings, Lucy, Ryan's wife, kept me updated on their healing progress.

Cassie's Healing Stories: Grief Can Cause Sickness and Suffering

In Cassie's first healing session, I invited my Higher Self and Ascended Master Kuthumi to send healing energy to her. The focus of this session was to heal Cassie's seizures. I instantly felt a lot of heat when I connected to her. Even the pet parent shared Cassie felt warm to the touch. We cleared the excess heat until Cassie's body cooled down significantly. Toward the end of the session, more heat was released from her body. After receiving the healing, Lucy shared that Cassie's body remained cooled down.

In her second healing session, there was intense pain around her heart, as if something physical was putting pressure on it. We released this pain which in turn released excess heat from her body. I felt the presence of another dog and saw it was trying to make a connection with Cassie. We cleared energetic blockages that surfaced from her throat chakra until the pressure at her heart completely dissipated. I was able to feel relief and joy in Cassie. Her energy was significantly lighter compared to at the start of the session. After the session, I asked Lucy if Cassie had experienced death, specifically of another dog. Lucy shared that Cassie had five puppies six years ago, and three of them died. Ryan tried to remove the dead puppies, but she held on to them, not wanting to let go. I hoped that during the healing session, one of her pups could connect with Cassie and give her closure and a sense of peace.

In her final healing session, numerous energetic blockages popped up. Once they were cleared, I could feel fresh life-force energy flowing into Cassie's body. There was pain in her lower jaw and emotional pain associated with that physical pain. Once the pain was cleared, I felt so much joy within her. I saw her running around in a forest, playing, and catching Frisbee. I checked in with Lucy about the pain in Cassie's jaw. My thought was she had an accident that injured her jaw. Lucy shared that her face was kicked in by a wild horse.

Weena's Healing Stories: A Pet Can Absorb Their Pet Parents' Pain, and They Might Suffer For It

In Weena's first healing session, the focus of the session was to heal vaginal bleeding as well as her reproductive system. I discovered there were energetic blockages around her rear area, and so I cleared the blockages. I sensed emotional pain; specifically, heartbreak coming up from her heart. There was also deep emotional pain, as if she had endured a lot. I teared up during this session because I felt her pain. I also allowed for the emotional pain to flow and released it. Her heart felt heavy like a stone and became lighter after her pain was cleared. After this session, Ryan shared that she looked happy when they went for a morning walk. I found out after this session that the heartbreak and deep emotional pain were not her own. They were Ryan's. Weena had absorbed these pains into her body and energetic field in her attempt to heal Ryan as he went through heart-breaking and challenging life experiences.

In her second healing session, there were energetic blockages in her throat chakra, and emotional pain came up from her heart. Her heart felt heavy because of it. After the energetic blockages and emotional pain were cleared, I felt the energy of peace being transmitted to Weena. Her heart felt significantly lighter afterward. I was able to feel happiness and eagerness in Weena. It felt like she was ready to live again and have lots of fun.

In her final healing session, the energy of sorrow came up. It weighed heavily on her heart and her whole body as if she could no longer bear it. I saw her lying on her side and felt she wanted to give up. I teared up again because the sorrow was too much. I asked my Higher Self and Ascended Master Kuthumi to clear the sorrow. I felt it dismantle bit by bit, and the intensity lessened. After this healing, both Lucy and Ryan noticed that Weena perked up again. She was not mopey and lethargic like before. Her vaginal bleeding seemed to have lessened and was less pungent compared to before.

Cassie and Weena are the first two animals that I have healed. In healing them, I have discovered that my Higher Self and I can heal animals. I also learned that pets can and are willing to absorb their pet parents' unresolved, unprocessed, suppressed emotions in their attempt to heal their pet parents. They do this because they love their pet parents unconditionally. They are like a child who is willing to take on their parents' pain and suffering so their parents can be happy and healthy. Unfortunately, when a loving pet takes in their pet parents' pain and suffering, it is often to their detriment.

I also notice that once energetic blockages in the chakras are cleared and emotional pains are released from the pets' energetic system, the pets tend to be a lot happier, become more energetic, and show up confident being themselves.

Conclusion

Since the healing session, Cassie has been doing better. She is a lot more active than usual. She also looks more alert and more alive. Her body temperature has dropped and is not as hot as before.

Weena's unconditional love for Ryan is very evident. Ryan is indeed very lucky and blessed to have received so much love and energetic support from Weena. Lucy shared that she believed that Weena's unconditional love for Ryan had saved him and kept him alive despite battling through tough life circumstances. She also shared that she felt the knock-on effect of Weena's healing. It felt very much like a release for all of them. Lucy felt that Weena was so blessed to have received the healing and all who are connected to Weena. She loved how the healing unfolded for everyone in her family. She shared that she recently discovered that Ryan's ex had a hysterectomy and came out of the hospital. She felt that Weena's bleeding was paralleling his ex's experience. She shared that she was surprised when Weena's vaginal bleeding lessened. It was in tandem with Ryan's ex's hysterectomy. She felt that Weena might have needed a hysterectomy like Ryan's ex, but because Weena took the energetic healing route, the need for surgery was circumvented.

Kash and Sammy's Healing Stories

Meet Kash and Sammy. They were stray cats and lived outdoors for the first three months of their lives. They were fed and cared for by a Muslim family. By the time they were three months old, they were rescued by a married couple. From there, they became indoor cats. Kash was an introverted cat, while Sammy was an anxious cat.

They are siblings and have never been apart from each other since they were born, until one fateful day when Sammy went missing. The cat sitters and pet parents were looking for Sammy all over the house and the surrounding areas. They also checked with nearby neighbors. Sammy was nowhere to be found. In the evening, Kash could not stop meowing as it was his first time being away from Sammy.

More than a week later, one of the cat sitters heard a commotion in the next house. She checked, and to her delight she saw Sammy. Her husband and their neighbor managed to catch him and returned him to his pet parents. Sammy was extremely skinny and hungry. The pet parents knew that Sammy underwent massive stress and trauma. They could see that he was still in survival mode with high anxiety. He was very distant and not relaxed since he was back. They also knew that Kash had missed Sammy so much because of his non-stop loud yowling.

Both pet parents agreed Kash and Sammy should receive energy healing. Each received a total of six sessions, twice a week for three weeks.

Kash's Healing Story: From Careful and Guarded to Open and Playful

During Kash's first session, the energy of sorrow came up. There was pain around the heart area and intense pressure at the sternum. Due to the intensity of the sorrow and pain at the heart, these were very slow to clear. Once they were cleared, intense pressure on the sternum was released, which helped him to feel relaxed and at ease.

On his third healing session, we cleared negative energy from his cells and energetic field. A deeper wound was revealed and felt very much like a child's wound. Something traumatic might have happened to him when he was younger, which could explain his introverted nature. The pet parent also noticed that Kash was isolating himself more, which had always been true even before Sammy went missing.

On his fourth healing session, I felt Kash's heart was open. I saw an image of him looking out from a hiding place. It seemed he was deciding when he wanted to "come out of his shell." We cleared emotional pain from his heart, allowing fresh life-force energy to fill his entire body. The pet parent could see a lot of improvement in Kash. He was more active than usual.

During his final healing session, I encountered a stubborn, energetic blockage deep in his throat. I had to "dive" in deep to clear this blockage. I saw I was diving deep into an ocean, and I saw a rusty plug at the bottom of the ocean floor. I pulled that plug out. Then I felt life-force energy flowing into his body. After the stubborn blockage was cleared, I saw Kash was very active and entertaining himself by playing with a toy.

Before Kash received energy healing, he was guarded and kept to himself.

After the final healing session, he became very open and playful. The pet parents noticed Kash approached them more for cuddles, and he loved being petted.

Sammy's Healing Story: Tearing Down the Wall

During Sammy's first healing session, I invited my Higher Self and Ascended Master Kuthumi to send healing energy to him. We encountered several energetic blockages during the session. Eventually I felt a blockage crack that released much trapped emotional energy. I then realized that this blockage was more of a wall. This blockage would interrupt energy flowing through channels while the wall was all around. I felt that Sammy might have created it for self-protection. Through the cracked wall, I could see the other side of Sammy that he kept hidden, which was a confident cat. After receiving the first healing session, Sammy was doing much better, and he was more energetic.

On his third healing session, Sammy was open and very receptive. It felt like he enjoyed receiving healing energy. In this session we cleared physical and emotional pain and grief. After this session the pet parent could see a huge difference with Sammy. He was more relaxed and less anxious. He was more open, playful, and loving than when he first came back.

On his fourth healing session, Sammy was very receptive. I felt so much joy and bubbliness within him. His body was filled with fresh life-force energy. I saw an image of him being very active and lively. We cleared several emotional pains that came up from his heart.

During his final healing session, Sammy was like a sponge. He soaked up all the healing energy. We also cleared physical and emotional pain. Toward the end of the healing session, I saw Sammy was very pleased with himself.

Before Sammy received energy healing, he never liked being held, cuddled, or picked up.

After the final healing session, Sammy would just hop onto his mommy's lap, ask to be picked up like a baby, and sleep in his mommy's arms like a sleeping baby. His pet parents could see a massive difference with Sammy and were so happy that he was more open to cuddles and very energetic now.

Conclusion

Sammy has been more relaxed and affectionate toward his brother, Kash. Kash would hop on the pet parents' lap to ask for cuddles.

When the pet parents watch TV, Sammy and Kash would come to them, sit, and hang around them instead of doing their own thing. Both have craved more attention from the pet parents. The pet parents also love the attention they get from Sammy and Kash. Previously, whenever Sammy wanted attention, Kash would be a few steps behind and stay quiet. Now Kash joins in and knows how to get the pet parents' loving attention.

Sammy and Kash are now two playful cats. They have become more loving toward the pet parents since receiving the healing. The joy and love they exude brings them closer to their pet parents. The pet parents undeniably feel more connected to them, and Sammy and Kash's joy and happiness add so much "richness" to the pet parents' lives.

Sven and Baxter's Healing Stories

Sven and Baxter are stray dogs currently under Natalie's care. Both dogs have skin issues. Sven continues to have skin issues despite taking his medication. Baxter had a skin issue since he was a young puppy. His skin issues come back intermittently even though his diet is watched carefully.

Sven's Healing Story: Loner Dog Becomes the Pack Leader

Sven had received a total of six healing sessions. The focus of his healing was physical body healing.

In his first healing session, my Higher Self and Ascended Master Kuthumi gave Sven an energetic cleansing bath. There was an energetic blockage in the throat chakra. We cleared the blockage, which revealed a much deeper one explaining why Sven had not fully recovered despite taking his medication. The blockage had prevented life-force energy from flowing into his body. Once we cleared some of the blockage, I could feel the life-force energy flowing into his body. I felt a space open up in his chest, allowing him to breathe deeper. There was also emotional pain around the heart area. It came up briefly and settled at the heart. At the end of the session, I was surprised to feel that he was tired or feeling lethargic. I mentioned it to Natalie, and she informed me that Sven had a history of heartworms.

In his third healing session, Sven was given an energetic cleansing bath. There was an energetic blockage in the throat chakra. After we cleared some of it, a heavy emotional pain was released from his heart. I saw Sven was slightly active and barking a lot. I also felt fresh life-force energy flowing into his body. Natalie confirmed that Sven had become more active. He would even growl and bark. He also enjoyed receiving extra attention from Natalie.

In his fourth healing session, Sven was given an energetic cleansing bath. There was an energetic blockage in the throat chakra. After we cleared some of it, the pressure on his heart was released. I saw Sven barking a lot. He was sitting tall and had regained his confidence. It looked like he was "standing his ground." We cleared more energetic blockages in the throat chakra, and I could feel fresh life-force energy flowing into his body. After this session, Natalie informed me that Sven was doing great. He was active and had become the pack leader. He was also growling and barking during mealtimes.

In his final healing session, a massive energy of heartache came up from his heart. After it was cleared, grief came up. It was flowing smoothly and released from his body. I felt his inner strength return. I asked Natalie if Sven was around a dog that died or if he knew a dog that died. Natalie mentioned that she rescued Sven with his female partner. He was very protective of her. Unfortunately, she passed away due to tick fever.

Before receiving this healing, Sven was a loner and kept to himself. Natalie shared that Sven most likely had a hard life before he was rescued. Sven and his significant other were abandoned by their previous owner and were still wearing collars from their previous owner.

After receiving this healing, Sven is more active and expresses himself by growling and barking. He no longer keeps to himself and instead has become the pack leader. His skin is fully recovered. Natalie was amazed at how different Sven is now compared to before.

Baxter's Healing Story: Becoming Baxter 2.0

Baxter had received a total of fourteen healing sessions. The focus of his healing was physical body healing.

In his first healing session, I asked my Higher Self and Ascended Master Kuthumi to heal Baxter's skin. There was emotional pain that came up from his heart. It was abandonment. There was also an energetic blockage in the throat chakra. After the emotional pain was released and the blockage cleared, he breathed better and deeper. I felt a lot of heat from his body, and the excess heat was released. I also felt life-force energy flowing into his body.

Unfortunately, his skin condition somehow worsened after Baxter's second healing session. His entire body was itchy with red raw rashes. This prompted me to do healing twice a week for him from then onwards. I also recommended Natalie bring him to see a vet.

After Baxter received four more healing sessions, he scratched less, and only some areas of his skin were slightly raw.

There were energetic blockages in the throat and heart chakras in his sixth healing session. We cleared as much as possible until I could feel cool life-force energy flowing into his body. An entity also enveloped his whole body, which we then cleared. We further cleared several emotional pains that came up from his heart. After the clearing, Baxter's heart became significantly lighter. I was able to feel joy within Baxter. I felt his heart was open. It felt like he had so much love to give and deserved love in return. I saw him walking, wagging his tail, and barking. I mentioned to Natalie that he might be slightly active, and his demeanor might change slightly. Natalie confirmed that Baxter was walking and wagging his tail. He was energetic and had been eating well.

In his seventh healing session, I could not feel him at first. His energy was too quiet. I saw him curl his body up and by himself. There were energetic blockages in both sides of Baxter's brain. After these blockages were cleared, I felt that Baxter perked up a bit. We cleared more energetic blockages in the throat and heart chakras. Then I saw him standing on all four legs and barking continuously. I felt his heart was lighter by the end of the session. I told Natalie that he might feel much better and more vocal than usual. He also might want to play with other dogs. Natalie was happy to report that Baxter was doing much better. He had started to mingle with the other dogs. His skin was not that raw anymore, but still bald and reddish.

In his eleventh healing session, I felt there were still energetic blockages in the throat and heart chakras. Fear and heartache surfaced from his heart as well. After we cleared the blockages and released the fear and heartache, I felt happiness in Baxter. I was able to feel cool life-force energy flowing into Baxter's body. I also felt some of his organs were lethargic. We cleansed his organs, and right after, I felt his organs were energized by the life-force energy. I felt his energetic field became younger. It was as if he received an upgrade, like Baxter 2.0. I felt he might be pumped and excited after receiving this healing. I saw he was active and playful. His heart was significantly lighter by the end of the session. Natalie confirmed that Baxter had become more active and energetic. He had been running around and playing with other dogs.

In his final session, there was a slight energetic blockage in the throat chakra. This energetic blockage was cleared. I could feel Baxter's body flooded with fresh life-force energy. I also felt his excitement. He might have become more energetic after receiving this healing. I could feel that his energetic field was cleared of any energetic blockages. I mentioned to Natalie that Baxter's body can heal itself if his energetic field is clear of energetic blockages.

Before receiving this healing, Baxter had kept to himself, and he was also weak due to his recurring skin issues.

After receiving a total of fourteen healing sessions, Baxter is doing great. His skin is not raw anymore, and his fur is growing back. He is more active, energetic, and mischievous too. He now mingles, plays, and runs around with other dogs. Natalie was delighted that Baxter had opened up to the other dogs, and she could see that Baxter was a lot happier now.

Conclusion

Natalie has such a big heart. Her love for animals led her to volunteer to rescue injured strays. She currently cares for more than fifty stray dogs and several abandoned puppies and kittens at her own home. She used to worry about Sven, Baxter, and other strays under her care that were somehow unable to fully recover from an injury or a disease. Now that Sven and Baxter are fully recovered, and the other strays are on their way to recovery, she feels a lot of relief. She no longer worries about them, and she can focus her energy on rescuing other injured stray animals and feeding a hundred-plus strays every single day. She is grateful that the healing has greatly impacted her strays' recovery and overall well-being.

Stacy and Darren's Healing Stories

Meet Stacy and Darren. They have been married for two years. Stacy is working in a local government job, while Darren recently got a job working overseas. They are now in a long-distance relationship, and it is their first time living apart from one another. They have been living apart for three months and are still adjusting, which both find difficult. Each has received a total of eight healing sessions over four weeks.

Stacy's Healing Story: From Mistrust to Empathy

In her first session, I asked my Higher Self to send healing energy to Stacy. There was an energetic blockage in the throat chakra and emotional pain around the heart area. We cleared the blockage and released the emotional pain. I discovered there was a deeper energetic blockage deep in the throat area. This blockage was connected to the left brain, and it was cleared. I could feel her heart was open, and love was flowing effortlessly. However, more energetic blockages surfaced from the throat chakra. These blockages were connected to the right brain and were cleared. At the end of the session, more emotional pain came up from her heart and was released. After this session, Stacy noticed that she and her husband texted more than usual. She also felt more loving toward her husband.

In her fourth session, Stacy wanted to work on her mental clarity. There was a massive energetic blockage in the throat chakra. A deeper blockage in the throat area was cleared as we cleared the blockage. It also cleared the right side of the brain and then the left side. After the clearing, I sensed she might feel some form of relief. There was a slight pain in the right shoulder blade, and this pain was released. We continuously cleared the energetic blockage in the throat chakra until I could feel cool life-force energy flowing into her body. I felt the energy of excitement within her. An energetic blockage in the heart chakra took a while to clear. After this session, Stacy shared that her sadness has reduced. She did not feel as sad as before. Her mental clarity and self-confidence improved. She did not second guess herself; she did not stumble looking for words, and they were flowing out of her effortlessly even though she was not feeling her best that day.

In her seventh session, Stacy wanted to work on her marriage. There were energetic blockages in the throat and heart chakras. These blockages were cleared. There was an energy that came up showing she was holding herself back from saying what she wanted to say. There was pain in her right shoulder blade. This pain was released. Throughout the session, we focused on clearing the throat chakra. There were some stubborn energies in the throat chakra. These energies were crystallized in the throat chakra. As we cleared them, I could feel that her mind had become calmer. I felt she might have more clarity after those crystallized energies were cleared. After this session, Stacy shared that she felt calmer and more at peace.

In her final session, Stacy wanted to continue to work on her marriage. There were energetic blockages in the throat and heart chakras. As we cleared the throat area, it also cleared the center part of her brain. I encountered several stubborn energies in the throat chakra. These energies were cleared. I also felt a lot of heat was released. I could feel her mind start to quiet down, and then clarity emerged. Throughout this session, we mostly cleared old thoughts from the throat chakra. I could feel her heart was lighter, and her mind was way less crowded. After this session, Stacy shared that she was less reactive. She took more time to step back and process her thoughts before coming down with any conclusions.

Before receiving this healing, Stacy had difficulty trusting her husband after he made a few mistakes in their marriage. Her inability to trust him developed into an insecurity that he would make those mistakes again even though she knew he had changed. The sad and angry thoughts pertaining to the distrust would intensify usually a week before her period, when her hormones were all over the place. Her feelings would overwhelm her, and this in turn would develop into arguments and fights. She also harbored resentment towards her husband due to his past mistakes. Because of her resentment, she did not have patience with him and would snap at her husband whenever he was upset with her or at something else.

Stacy also felt that her self-confidence was low. She found herself being self-critical, having self-doubt, and fearing people's judgments. She would write something, and then a few minutes later she would delete what she wrote. These are the things that she has never done before. She had a lot of worries, constant ruminations, and over-thinking. She felt that she was stuck mentally. She shared that she had a brain fog which caused forgetfulness and difficulty finding the right words to say and write.

During the course of receiving this healing, Stacy and her husband had a couple of fights. In one of their fights, Stacy quickly realized that "being right" was not important even though it was convenient for her to do so. Stacy chose to apologize and took responsibility for her actions. She also consoled her husband, which helped him to soften up and eventually no longer be upset. She realized that not all battles have to be won. Or rather, not all battles have to be fought.

After receiving these healing sessions, she noticed that even though the distrust is still present, it is not as intense as before. She can manage the thoughts that come with the distrust. She can reason and challenge those thoughts. Any residual anger and sadness are not as intense. She also noticed that she no longer harbors any resentment toward her husband and is now more empathetic towards him.

She processes things faster, including her thoughts, emotions, new ideas, and things happening around her. She is more confident in her writing. She surprises herself when she becomes more creative and develops new ideas and plans. She knows what actions she needs to take to plan for her future and even what she needs to do the next day. She no longer ruminates and overthinks as much. Even though her worries are still present, she no longer allows herself to overthink. Stacy shared that even though some parts of her brain are still foggy, the good news is the thick fog has lifted. For her, changes are happening on a smaller scale, but she now notices how different she feels and thinks. She is completely amazed by how much she has changed in just four weeks.

Darren's Healing Story: Being Bottled Up Stresses You Out

In his first session, I asked my Higher Self to send healing energy to Darren. There were energetic blockages in the throat and heart chakras. Fear about marriage came up as well. The energetic blockages and fear were cleared. I could feel the energy of calmness wash over Darren, but it was brief. I felt the energy of anger surface, and it was released. More fears about marriage came up, and they were cleared. There was pain in his left lung and at the back of his left lung, which was released. I felt more clearing happening in both the throat and heart chakras.

In his second session, Darren wanted to work on his marriage. There was an energetic blockage in the throat chakra. As we cleared the throat chakra, life-force energy flowed into his body. It flowed to the left side of the body first, focusing more on the left leg and then the right side of the body. I informed him that he might feel tingly all over or cold. I also felt that he might have the courage to speak up. Throughout the session, we focused on clearing his throat chakra. I felt a lot of heat release from the throat chakra and the whole body, which is a good sign because that meant stagnant energy was released. The next day, Darren shared that he and his wife actually fought the night after each of their healing sessions. But interestingly, he shared that he found it was easier to say what was on his mind rather than bottling it up and keeping quiet about it. After their argument settled, where he expressed himself more openly, he felt at ease and no longer stressed out.

Darren wanted to work on anger management and clarity in his sixth session. There were energetic blockages in the throat chakra. We cleared these blockages. I was able to feel that his throat was open. Then the energy moved to clear his solar plexus chakra. I saw a seed of anger that grew into a rotten tree bark in his solar plexus chakra. This energy was cleared. The energy moved again to clear his throat chakra. I felt a very old energy embedded deep in his throat chakra. I saw this energy was from a very old woman. This energy had been passed down from her to Darren. This energy might have shaped how he viewed and thought about things and the world in general. We cleared this energy. As a result, a lot of residual energy came out, as if we opened up a can of worms. Throughout this session, we oscillated between clearing the solar plexus and the throat chakras. I felt that Darren's views and thoughts of the world might change after this session. The next day Darren shared that he felt clearer and less burdened.

In his final session, Darren wanted to work on his marriage. There were energetic blockages in the throat and heart chakras. There were several pains that came up from his heart. The blockages were cleared, and the pains were released. A lot of heat was released while clearing the throat and heart chakras. I was able to feel life-force energy flowing into Darren's body. I felt an old energy embedded in his throat chakra. I saw this energy was from his father. This energy shaped how Darren showed up in the world. This energy was cleared. I felt that Darren might feel a bit different after this healing. I felt his heart becoming lighter, and there was space in his chest. I felt his sinuses might clear up, and he could breathe more easily.

Before receiving the healing, Darren found it hard to express himself. He feared that he would say the wrong thing as he did not want to trigger his wife. He was also worried that his marriage might fall apart.

During the healing sessions, Darren had a lot of things going on in his life. He was moving to a new apartment, and he was also busy with the opening of his restaurant. Being away from his wife had not made it easier for him to juggle work, moving into a new home, and working on their relationship. Hence, he felt that he was pushed to his limit and almost became immobilized like he used to be before.

After receiving the healing, Darren is calmer than before. He says and discusses things as they come up. He no longer bottled up his emotions. He is now confident and takes a different approach to handling things at work and in his personal life.

Conclusion

Stacy shares that since she and her husband received the healings, their communication has improved immensely! Previously they would usually drag their fights out for days, followed by extended periods of the silent treatment. However, now she notices that her husband is getting better at communicating his needs, emotions, and feelings with her. This leads to their fights resolving quicker, and sometimes within a few hours. Stacy was surprised at how much the healing had helped them.

Darren now communicates better with his wife, which in turn improves his communication with his team and his boss at work. He also did the impossible thing in less than three weeks after being hired. He soft-launched his restaurant and got supplies during

Chinese New Year when suppliers are on a long holiday. He is handling things better and can see things differently from before. He also loves his wife, even more so than before and without doubt.

Moving Forward

Becoming the Being of Light that we truly are takes complete honesty with ourselves and the willingness to heal. As humans, we have lived for so many years in this world, and each of us is far from perfect. Most of us may still have unresolved trauma, whether sexual in nature or otherwise. Unresolved grief and loss are also common, either from the death of loved ones or the end of important relationships. Unresolved issues often repeatedly return to us until we have learned and resolved our lessons.

After practicing energy healing for more than a decade, I discovered there are layers upon layers that need clearing and healing. Even though I have left the cycle of rebirth and passed the sixth initiation, I find clearing and healing is a never-ending process. We can always go deeper when healing ourselves through energy healing, especially with Higher Self's assistance. The Higher Self is capable of miraculous healing.

Invitation: Heal Your Heart

Have you gone through grief, loss, or heartbreak and not yet dealt with them? If so, my Higher Self is encouraging you to heal your heart. The heart is the source of our love for ourselves, other people, and other beings. When energetic blockages are present in the heart chakra, this often shows up as the lack of self-love, difficulty forgiving oneself or other people, and lack of compassion. When the heart chakra is free from energetic blockages, the heart chakra is awakened and open to love and to receive love in return. Accessing unconditional love, forgiveness, compassion, and other higher emotions is also easier. If you feel that you have heart-related trauma and you are ready to heal your heart, embody love, and raise your vibration, start your healing journey with us.

For more information about Heal Your Heart, go to www.powercreatefreedom.com.

Invitation: Healing for Pets and Animals

Just like humans, animals also have an energetic system. Hence, animals can also benefit tremendously from energy healing. Having healed many animals, both pets and strays, I find animal transformation through energy healing both fascinating and rewarding. Energy healing with my Higher Self, Yestred, and Ascended Master Kuthumi will help to heal your pet's physical body, accelerate their recovery, and boost their energy levels. Energy healing can complement veterinary care if you have pets with recurring physical issues. If your pets are stressed or depressed or experience trauma or grief, energy healing can help restore their happiness, confidence, and enthusiasm. Energetically healthy pets often show up as physically and emotionally healthy pets. So much more is possible as pets and animals receive healing from Yestred and Ascended Master Kuthumi. Find out the state of your pets' energetic health and improve it by trying out Healing for Pets and Animals today.

For more information about Healing for Pets and Animals, go to www.powercreatefreedom.com.

Invitation: Support Healing for Strays

My Higher Self, Yestred, and I are healing stray animals daily. We used to heal stray animals once a week, but it has evolved into daily healing. This project was born out of love for animals and the desire for strays to live happier and healthier lives. In this healing, my Higher Self would gather stray animals from all over the world, focusing on those that need healing. We have done a lot of healing, ranging from healing for injured strays to strays that are near the end of their life.

Energy healing can help hasten their recovery, reveal their personality, release their pain, and alleviate their suffering.

I invite you to support this project. For more information, head over to Healing for Strays on our website, www.powercreatefreedom.com.

Hayatti Rahgeni, Brunei, Borneo

Be our Patron: www.patreon.com/hayattirahgeni

Subscribe to our YouTube: www.youtube.com/powercreatefreedom

Follow our Instagram: www.instagram.com/powercreatefreedom

Like our Facebook Page: www.facebook.com/powercreatefreedom

Chapter Three

Embodying the Priestess
Turning Pain into Power

by
Charlene Locke

Your body is a sacred vessel of light, each one precious and unique.

-Valkarin Sixth Ray Priestess

Personal Life Ascension Journey

My unique path to ascension came from deep lessons, painful shedding, letting go, heartbreak, and rising from the ashes of what I thought life should look like.

In short, at twenty-eight I fell in love with someone who just casually walked into where I worked one day. I had never experienced such gravitation before. My stomach literally flipped; every part of me knew this person, yet I had never laid eyes upon him. I had this strange sentence come into my mind. I have never forgotten the words, "Thank goodness I have found you again." I remember being really perplexed as to why I would think such a strange thought.

At this point in my life, I was married to a beautiful, kind, and caring soul. We had a home and a lovely life together. Inexplicably, I made the decision to turn my back on absolutely everything. None of my decisions made any sense at that time, yet there was a force propelling me forward. Within months I was pregnant with my daughter. Without a doubt, this was probably one of the hardest times of my life. The judgment I received from others for many years after was unprecedented. I was alone and scared and about to journey into motherhood with what felt like no stability or support.

But remarkably, what was becoming increasingly apparent was that, spiritually, I was awakening at a rapid pace.

My daughter Chloe and I were already incredibly connected. I call her, "my gift from Venus." I could sense her soul even a few days before conception. Together we have journeyed for many millennia. She has been my twin in a previous life, a sister, a teacher, and a fellow priestess in others. As soon as we were energetically connected again in this life, it was like a light bulb illuminating my intuition. I started to receive much clearer images of spirit animals and guides. Her arrival ushered in a new energy; one of remembering.

Our life for many years was not easy. My heart sometimes felt like it was in a million pieces. Her father and I had many contracts and life lessons to learn together that stretched over many lives. The words I heard so clearly on meeting him were so true. I had found him again. In another life, he had left, and I had spent many years looking for him. We had so many cords that even when he was not with me, I could sense him. This was incredibly painful, for I knew he wasn't as loyal to me as I was to him. I was left as a single mother in the ashes of what I thought life would look like.

But yet again, I was being pushed by spirit to rise; to delve deeply into my karmic debt, to look at my past lives, old vows, and contracts and begin to ascend. And ascend I did! I developed a much deeper relationship with my guides and Ascended Masters. Each one supported my life and my work. This is how my "embodying the priestess" began the journey to my Higher Self.

Without a doubt, the birth of my daughter forced me to awaken, stand in my power, and relive many painful tests and lessons. It forced me to turn inward to a strength I didn't believe I had in earlier years. Now with a deeper understanding, my Higher Self gave me a potent message for Motherhood:

> "We, the Priestesses, whisper to you to rise, dear sister. As a mother, you birth a new generation. Teach her the old ways, show her the Earth and Sky, and in turn she will show us all on Earth what harmony and joy truly are. Your path will pave the way to show others that a mother's intuition is one of the strongest forces on earth. This is part of your journey to embodying the priestess."

As it stands today, my Higher Self is fully anchored within my holy heart, and we have together, in this life, embodied the priestesses. There was no huge ceremony or announcing it from the rooftops. I just had a quiet inner knowing that we had merged to a state of unity and oneness and that we were to share the golden codes of the ancient priestesses to re-awaken and re-activate all that felt the call to journey with us.

Professional Life

Alongside my personal Ascension journey, I have been a holistic therapist for over twenty years. In this life, I have re-learned ancient practices such as Sekhem Reiki, Crystal Healing, Aromatherapy,

Facials, Reflexology, Massage, Sound Healing, Yoga, and Breathwork. This gives me an opportunity within healings to synergistically bring different practices together for deep transformation. Many of my past lives had been within healing spaces, from the temples of Egypt to the Pleiadian Light Temples.

My Higher Self explains that we must harness multiple practices within our sessions to treat both the physical and spiritual bodies together to get to the root cause of what we are working on. She explains that as the Earth is shifting frequency and evolving, so must we. We must move forward from old programs, patterns, and beliefs. Now more than ever, we must connect with the earth and nature and fully understand how connected we all are.

Many of our teachings and healings use frequency, plants, and natural resources, all designed to bring equilibrium and balance. Our bodies and our minds are capable of the most incredible transformation, but first we must re-learn that the power and remedy are not external to us. It has been within us all along.

My Higher Self and I offer Group Retreats, Temple Journeys, and One to One Hands-on therapies holding space for those ready to unlock their true potential.

Higher Self

So, you may be wondering, who is My Higher Self? Her name is Valkarin, and she is a Golden Ray Priestess. She is on the sixth ray of devotion and of the goddess.

If Valkarin were to stand before you, you would see she has very long hair. Her eyes are golden, and she wears what looks like a golden bodice. She has a huge pair of golden wings that trail behind her. Her wings are used in two ways: one, to shield and surround the recipient in love; or two, for energetically transporting a soul to many of the healing temples she has access to in our world and other star systems. She calls these temple healings.

In her left hand is a jewelled sword. She refers to this not as a weapon but as a strong talisman for healing. Her sword emits emerald light codes designed for her to unlock and activate those she is working on within a healing session. Her energy is powerful, yet with incredible softness. She has a great love for all beings.

Valkarin is a descendant of the ancient Valkyrie. To honour this life, she appears sometimes with a huge white-winged horse, depending on the energy she wishes to bring forth. In this form, she works closely with Freya and Odin, who she explains are part of her soul group. In this form, she brings through the energy of runes, crystals, and plant medicine to bring forth deep healing and transformation. She explains why, in history, there is a memory of Odin's Valkyrie as they were the healers and the carriers of souls who appeared to help all those in need. However, this isn't the only form she appears in. She also has energetic connections with other ancient civilisations. Her appearance also shows her as an Egyptian Priestess. She has served in many temples and sacred places in this form. She holds a staff; the staff activates healing, light, and energy codes. In this form, she works closely with Isis, Anubis, and Sekhmet. In this form, she mostly works in ceremony weaving and alchemising with sound healing and frequency, bringing in an intuitive hands-on approach to healing through Reflexology, Sound Healing, and Breathwork.

Her different abilities are what make her a Master Healer. Although she prefers the term Energy Alchemist!

Together we can connect with Guides, Ascended Masters, Archangels, and Cosmic Healing Temples.

Client: Katie, age twenty-four

Client Concern: Painful and debilitating monthly cycles

Session Type: Physical Body Healing, Crystal Grid Healing, Sacred Reflexology, Sekhem Reiki, Womb Healing

Katie came to me at the age of twenty-four. She was suffering from problems with her monthly cycles. She had been placed on the contraceptive pill at age sixteen as a recommendation from her family doctor due to severe pain and heavy bleeding. But she was still suffering from monthly fatigue, pain, and discomfort year by year, and it was steadily getting worse. We decided to energetically body scan. This is a method I use to look at the body in more detail. I'm looking for subtle clues, blockages, or signals of what's happening at a deeper level. Immediately I was brought to the ankle, where a nasty break occurred at age seven. As we moved up the body, we began to see in more detail how we could help.

I was guided to use clear Quartz pieces all over the abdomen. We got started straight away on carrying out Sekhem Reiki & Reflexology. In reflexology terms, the break in the ankle was right on the fallopian tube and uterus. This was affecting the entire flow of energy to the womb space. Now mixed with years of worry and fear, it directly impacted Katie's physical body, so we cleared patterns of pain, dread, and even loathing of the body; followed by a guided meditation and visualisations for deep womb healing.

A fortnight later, Katie called me in shock. She had her first cycle where there was a noticeable difference. After a series of sessions, there is no heavy bleeding or pain, and Katie has regained the connection with the incredible power of her womb space, giving her body balance and reconnection. Blockages, breaks, and old wounds can have a significant impact on the entire balance of the body. Her body had been signalling that something was out of alignment for years. We just needed to tune in and listen to what it was trying to tell us.

Client: Ben, age thirty-five

Client Concern: Snowboarding injury to the lower leg, leading to several surgeries. Now unable to walk without crutches, leading to severe depression

Session Type: Multiple modalities

Ben was referred to me by a family member. When he arrived, he was incredibly skeptical. To him, I was some strange crystal-wielding woman, talking about energies and spirits. I could tell he was in a hurry to leave! I asked whether I could take a look, as this was a complex injury; one which was having a severe impact on Ben's mental health. He had been having very dark moments of not wanting to be here, had been unable to play sports or sleep properly, and was in constant pain. His energy was low.

He permitted me to start a gentle guided meditation, followed by a sound healing session. We journeyed together through the frequencies of our gongs, Quartz crystal bowls, and tuning forks; Valkarin weaving her magic around the body. Within fifteen minutes, Ben had fallen asleep! He continued to sleep for the rest of his session. This allowed what I like to call rest and reset, which gives us a chance to begin to work with the body at a much deeper level. Sound frequency can change cells within the body. Valkarin describes "Frequency" as the gateway to the cosmos; its medicine is far-reaching. Certain frequencies have different effects, so in Ben's case we needed to use a combination of sounds for cell renewal, nerve damage, and nullifying fear and discord.

A rather dazed Ben woke up. He smiled and looked at me. "Wow, that's the first time I've really relaxed in eight months."

"Great," I said. "Now we can get you healing from the inside out."

For four months, we worked together on Sound Healing, Past Life Clearing, Soul Retrieval, Morning Affirmations, Breathwork, and Visualisations. Our focus was on achieving the best possible outcome. We began to bring in elements of Kundalini Yoga, Aromatherapy, Massage, and Hands-on Healing.

Ben was incredibly dedicated to his path to healing. These deep sessions need a commitment at home to break through and discover the power within. In this case, Valkarin and I were there to hold space and give the tools needed. I'm happy to say that years later, Ben has overcome this injury, and for that, I'm incredibly proud of him.

Client: Claire, age fifty-six

Client Concern: Grief after the loss of a parent

Session Type: Angelic Reiki & Crystal Healing

Claire came to me after the loss of her mum. They had an incredibly close bond. Her death had been unexpected and a terrible shock. Overwhelmed, not sleeping, and exhausted, the loss significantly impacted every aspect of her life. Valkarin immediately stepped forward for this session with a team of Archangels: Michael, Gabriel, Uriel, and Raphael. They surrounded her entire body in a bubble of Divine Light. They wished for her to be held and loved. During the sessions, I was given the sight of a beautiful pure white rose, along with an image of an antique blue sapphire jewelled cross. We moved through the energetic bodies, clearing and cleansing old emotions to bring balance and harmony back to the entire energy system. We continued placing beautiful crystals all around the body—including Celestite, Selenite, and Kunzite—all working on heart healing, peace, and support. These are some of the most wonderful crystal energies to work with.

This allowed Claire to permit her body to surrender and rest for the first time in many months. So many tears were shed in that session, but throughout the entirety was the incredible team of Archangels. Each tear was alchemised into pure love.

Toward the end of the session, a message came through for Claire, "Darling, never forget, our love stretches across all time. Energy never ceases to exist; I am with you always."

When I sat Claire up at the session's end, I could see her eyes. They were sparkling. Each cell within her body had been flooded with divine love and light.

I told her about the images of the white rose and cross, and she laughed immediately. "Charlene," she said, "How could you have known this? My mum adored white roses, and this is her cross that she wore all the time. I have it now in my jewellery box at home." Our ancestors and family, in my experience, always give little symbols or messages that are only relevant to us. A little confirmation they are there with us always.

Grief, I believe, comes in waves. Sometimes we notice it more than others, and on days when we feel out of our depth, these sessions are a way of navigating and releasing our emotions so we may move forward knowing we are loved and supported.

Client: Lauren, aged thirty-eight

Client Concerns: Severe Migraines

Session Type: Water Healing Temple

Lauren came to me suffering from severe migraines, having tried everything. She was recommended to book a session with me to see what we could do.

This was a magical unfolding of not only physical body healing but of other lives, ancestral trauma healing, and the experience of energetically being taken to a healing temple by the priestesses. Over several sessions, we worked on clearing past lives of trauma that were directly impacting this one. The most fascinating part of one of the sessions was seeing Lauren in another life where she had suffered a severe head injury. It was a life with some truly traumatic experiences—from famine to war; the very energetic imprints had truly left their mark.

Stepping forward with Valkarin in this session were Ascended Masters Thoth, Anubis, Isis, and Sekhmet. We were taken to the point of origin in this past life. The blow to the head was so forceful it ended Lauren's life. We were asked to energetically place a golden protection grid over Lauren, clearing cellular memory of this event. After we had completed the healing, Lauren explained she was aware of pressure and tingling all over the head and coming down the side of her face. A clearing like this can take time for the energies to integrate, and Lauren was absolutely exhausted for a good twenty-four hours afterwards.

A few weeks later, we continued with another session. Valkarin explained we would be energetically taking Lauren to one of the many ancient water healing temples this time.

These sacred temples are used by the golden ray priestesses for unique energy upgrades and light code transmissions. Using sound frequency and visualisations, Valkarin began Lauren's journey. We arrived at the most beautiful stone steps where the ground was covered in snow and the air misty. The mist is steam coming from one of the ancient healing pools. Its appearance is that of a hot spring. During this healing transmission, Lauren's energetic bodies were bathed in the healing waters, held, and moved through the pool by the golden ray priestess. I was aware during this session that Ascended Master Freya stepped forward. This sacred pool has incredibly potent energies; each cell within the body is bathed with light codes unique to the recipient. During these sessions I am asked to energetically hold the physical room with sound, usually crystal bowls or gongs.

Once the priestesses were finished, the body was gently brought out of the water. At the top of the stone steps, Freya placed an energetic rune symbol into Lauren's hand. This I recognised to be the FEHU rune. Although there are many descriptions and interpretations of rune meanings, this was for Lauren, for replenishing energy. It was for health and rejuvenation. These can be placed on or around the body for additional healing and support. This gift from Freya was an energetic imprint to boost her life force energy.

Once these sessions were complete, Valkarin ensured all the bodies were aligned, grounded, and balanced as Lauren slowly came around from a blissful sleep, having received her Water Temple Healing.

These sessions provide healing across all spaces and dimensions. Their effects can be felt for some time afterwards.

Session Type: Group Temple Healings

Energetic Journey: Temple of Philae

Ascended Masters present: Isis, Valkarin, Sekhmet, Hathor, Ishtar

Valkarin explained to me that the need for group healings would increase over the years. I must admit this was something well out of my comfort zone.

I felt too shy to stand in front of a group of people, let alone tell them we were about to journey to the temple of Philae as we sat in our retreat space in the not-so-sunny UK! If anyone had said to me twenty years ago that this would not only be possible, but transformational for those in the room, I wouldn't have believed a word!

A few weeks before, Valkarin and Isis joined me during a meditation. They showed me the temple of Philae; its beautiful pillars, hieroglyphics, and the water of the Nile with its banks teeming with life. I remember smiling and soaking up all the energies. My happy place for as long as I can remember has always been on the banks of the Nile. I would close my eyes and see the water glistening, the sunrises, the wildlife, and my soul would feel at peace—a soul remembering being in service with Isis. But I digress...getting back to the Temple Healing!

Isis explained, "It is time." We would be taking a group of twelve to receive Light code healings from the goddesses and priestesses, and I would take these women through a guided ceremony first.

On the day of the Temple Retreat, the energies were high. I began intuitively making a crystal healing grid. This would be in the centre of the room, beaming out its magical frequencies. Crystal grids bring such potent energy to the room. This one was made with Lapis Lazuli, Blue Lotus, Hibiscus, Clear Quartz, and Carnelian.

We journeyed through a Blue Lotus tea ceremony, connecting everyone to their deep intuition and honouring all those who have worked with its medicine before. Continuing with the power of our breath, we began releasing and surrendering before we entered the temple of Philae. Each participant, lying cosy under their blankets in the retreat space, was energetically transported to the temple as I guided us through a visualisation of what was taking place.

Isis began talking in the softest light language, welcoming all to this temple. Her energy was radiant, like a great mother welcoming her children home. For many lifetimes, the priestesses had been waiting for this group of souls to return to the temple. One by one, each recipient received powerful downloads, clearances, and energetic upgrades not only from Isis, but from Sekhmet, Ishtar, and Hathor.

Toward the end of the ceremony, a Golden Ankh was placed into the heart space of all the attendees. These energetic symbols harness the power of deep transformation; once in place, they can be called upon for strength, protection, wisdom, and the remembrance that all is connected.

The energy within the temple was electric. Waves of light and sound swirled around. Each person received golden light and energy codes streaming through the crown, lighting up the entire chakra system.

Once the ceremony was completed, we were all energetically brought safely back to our cosy retreat space. Everyone's experience was so different within the temple. Some felt deep heart healing, another felt tears of joy to be held within the temple. One felt energy clearing from her throat chakra after years of blockages. Many participants experienced a deep sense of peace and remembering. Physical body sensations such as tingling and heat were also experienced.

But one thing was clear, this journey had been transformational on so many levels.

Philae was the beginning of our temple journey healings; since then, many more have been birthed.

Each temple has a unique frequency and a unique set of healing benefits. There are always more profound reasons for visiting. Valkarin has worked within and has access to many of these temples. I am told this is a great honour, as the keys to these temples are bestowed to only a few.

Some of my favourites are The Venus Star Temple, Sirius Forest Temple, Atlantean Aqua Temple, and the Temple of the Elohim.

Client: Sarah

Client Concern: Physical pain

Session Type: Sound and Crystal Healing; Venus Star Temple

Sarah came in with back and shoulder pain. We sat down together during the first session, and it was apparent there was more to these symptoms than met the eye.

Many of my clients who book an intuitive massage and sacred reflexology do not really know what to expect. Some are very skeptical of healings and—due to the circumstances they have been through—are really closed off. Sarah wouldn't mind me saying she was one of these people. Her sister had bought her a gift voucher, and she most definitely wasn't that keen on wanting me to start sound and crystal healing! There's a certain look I receive! Usually as if I have come from a different planet. But bless her, she got on the treatment bed, and we got to work.

Valkarin intuitively guides me in sessions to areas that are blocked or where the energy is trapped and stagnant. Our bodies are an intricate wonder. Each system interacts and responds to not just our physical body, but our emotional and mental bodies. Our body responds to each frequency we give out, each thought, emotion, and action. Over time these can build up, causing blockages. I see them in sessions as unique little road maps to the root of what your body is telling you. Perhaps the start was many years before, and your bodies were given subtle little clues. We push on, ignore, or mask it until the signal is less subtle, and we become frustrated with our pain or when an injury is not healing. Different areas of the body can relate to different emotions or patterns we are holding onto. During one-to-one sessions, we can journey through what the body is holding on to, see what needs releasing, and quietly listen to its inner wisdom... we are here to hold space for the recipient to heal and step into their power.

Returning to Sarah...her back, shoulder, and neck were really tense. We worked through stretches and gentle massage. But what was very clear at this point was that we needed to begin working on the heart and throat chakras. Both of these energy points were incredibly heavy. We glided through our massage, continuing to place our weighted tuning forks in key acupressure points all up the spine. Each tuning fork has a different frequency. Valkarin had chosen a frequency of 136Hz followed by 528Hz. These she calls our heart and mind repair. They allow a beautiful connection between the heart and mind, soothing any fears and past hurts to allow deeper states of relaxation within the body. We finished with a beautiful quartz crystal bowl sound healing leaving Sarah totally relaxed.

After that session, Sarah rebooked each time, becoming more open to what we could do for her. The massage and sound allow recipients to relax and know they are held and safe. It allows a gentle dropping of guards and protection we sometimes put around ourselves.

During one session, Valkarin expressed that it was time to delve deeper now. We would begin by clearing the old. Sarah's marriage had broken down the year before, and this was something she had really been struggling with. During her marriage she had found it difficult to communicate with her partner for fear of how he would react. She was struggling with how she looked and felt, and her heart had been broken. We talked about her childhood and teenage years right up to the present day. Unpacking together, we saw that these feelings were something she had struggled with even as a child.

These were patterns of low self-esteem, wanting to shrink into the background, and not feeling worthy of love and respect. We began a series of sessions from inner-child healing, to calling back her power, to revisiting events that had shaped her adult life, slowly clearing and allowing Sarah to reclaim her power. We began a series of affirmations for daily use, all based on love and self-worth.

I am worthy of healthy, loving relationships.

I choose to love myself as deeply as I love others.

My favourite session with Sarah was when Valkarin and Ascended Masters Aphrodite and Quan Yin journeyed energetically with Sarah to The Venus Star Temple. Who would have thought six months prior we could be embarking on such incredible journeys? It was safe to say Sarah now had first-hand experience of what was possible.

The Venus Star Temple is one of the most elaborate of the temples. Its doors are engraved with beautiful symbols and flowers, and its great hall is full of crystals. The domed ceiling is open to the bluest of skies. There's a sense of only love and joy here. The frequency of this temple can be felt immediately. It's the frequency of pure love and devotion. The Archangels and Elohim gather here. It's a place of deep connection and reverence.

Sarah was carefully placed on one of the many seats within the hall. She was asked to give permission for Aphrodite and Quan Yin to connect.

Moving forward first was the goddess Aphrodite. She embodied the essence of self-love, divine love, relationship love, and the love of your body. When working with anyone, she understands and feels everything their heart has been through. She placed her hand on Sarah's heart centre and asked her to release any concerns, heartache, and past hurts. She was to release and surrender. Pink and white light swirled all around the bodies releasing and clearing.

Floating towards Sarah next, on a beautiful lotus flower, was the Goddess Quan Yin, the goddess of grace, compassion, mercy, wisdom, and true enlightenment. She surrounded Sarah's heart in pure divine light so she could once again feel her own divine spark of light within her. The masters held her in love and joy, ensuring each cell within her body had been filled with light.

Once the session was complete, Sarah slowly began her descent back through the veil of light, being safely held in Valkarin's wings and transported back to her physical body and back to the present in our retreat space. Her heart chakra had received healing across all times, places, and dimensions...totally infused with pure love and light.

It was an honour to see such transformational healing.

Client: Amy

Client Concern: Lower back pain/coccyx pain

Session Type: Pleiadian Light Healing

Amy came to me with issues surrounding lower back and coccyx pain. She found it hard to manoeuvre after almost three and a half years of recurring pain.

For these types of physical body healings, we work with a Light being who refers to himself as "A Pleiadian Light Surgeon." Many Pleiadian beings are assisting humanity at this time, bringing in the frequencies of harmony and truth. His knowledge of the human body is vast; understanding each connection, tissue, and organ. His healing sessions are carried out with utmost precision and far more advanced light technology than we have here on Earth. He gets to work quickly with what is best described as a silver thread of light that he can work his way around the spine and coccyx, showing me areas of misalignment. Whilst he is working, we assist using a tuning fork of 50Hz. This particular frequency is excellent for nerve, bone, and connective tissue repair, followed by hands-on healing and intuitive massage. He showed me an image of a previous fall. The impact was directly on the coccyx. This originally caused a small fracture, which Amy confirmed with us. The Silver Light Energy was used to align, rebalance, and stabilise this area, providing the deep physical body healing it needed. There was no pain for Amy during the session despite what a deep level the light surgeon was working at. She was able to feel and sense heat around the lower back. He finished the session using frequency and light codes. They energetically fall all over the body in what looks like the most beautiful silver rain. A complete reset has taken place for Amy.

Frequency has been used to heal for thousands of years, and many other beings and planets use this technology to assist in injury repair. There is much that can be done alchemising these powerful frequencies that are available to us. Working with Valkarin and the Light Surgeon is an honour. They have much to reawaken and teach us.

These are just a few of our most memorable one-to-one and group healings.

Valkarin wanted me to finish our chapter with a reminder to all, no matter where you are on your healing journey.

> "Remember to be in the light means to face the Dark, and to face the Dark you must remember your origins are not of this world...you must remember your divinity. Our mission here on earth is to anchor the light, raise the vibration, and help you to remember your power. Never forget your power is not external to you. It is inside of you. We

are all one soul, one collective. Your frequency is of love and unity, and if you feel alone or out of your depth, remember there is a legion of Star Beings, Angels, and Masters rooting for your very existence. Reach out. I am here should you need me."

"Thank you for sharing our Ascension journey and most memorable Healings with us."

"I send you much love and light, Charlene."

"A se a n a tu an ekmen"

"We rise together."

Charlene Locke, United Kingdom and Luxor, Egypt

Retreats, Energy Alchemy and Group Sessions Worldwide

For Retreat information, Email: charlene@trinityretreats.com

Or Phone: +44 738 715-9102

For Energy Alchemy and Group Sessions,
Email: info@charlenelocke.com

Instagram: charlenelocke_energyalchemy

Facebook: Charlene Locke Energy Alchemy

Chapter Four

Your Home as Your Sanctuary

by Carol Anne Halstead

As above, so below. As within, so without. As the universe, so the soul.

Hermes

In this chapter I will explain how I came to the healing arts and the unique practice of Ascension Dowsing. You will read how powerful and positive the effects are for our clients worldwide.

I also compiled a book called *Modern Ascension,* published in 2020. There are thirteen stories in it written about the storytellers' Ascension paths. This book is a good read whether you are on a spiritual path or beginning to discover there is more to life on Earth. You will find the stories helpful in understanding the journey of Ascension.

My Path to the Healing Arts and Spiritual Awakening

My route to spiritual awakening came through an interest in healing when I was a young mom and nursing teacher several years ago. I became curious about energy healing, but I was working within a medical model, so I began to search for understanding elsewhere. I found books and articles written about healing. I learned about prayer circles. I studied how to use intention, visualization, color, and sound. I read about miraculous recoveries and the placebo effect. Here was healing that defied rational explanation. I wanted to know why.

I found a course I could attend on "Therapeutic Touch." Dr. Dolores Krieger was the nurse/scientist who developed this course. Her research showed that there was a scientific basis for healing. This was a pivot point for me; I experienced a paradigm shift within my mind which changed the course of my career. There was no going back.

During the course, I learned how to move my hands around a person's energy or auric fields. I had an opportunity to help my brother shortly after taking the course. John complained about how much his hands hurt. He was a project manager at an inner-city highway construction site and worked outside in the cold. I offered to practice the techniques I had learned. I could feel the heat emanating from his hands. I "smoothed out" the energy fields around both hands as I had been taught. I worked until the heat had dissipated and there was a coolness felt. John reported his hands felt better. The pain was gone. Over the next two months, he continued to work outdoors, but the pain in his hands did not return. Ever!

This opened my eyes to the possibilities that energy healing could create. At that time, most people around me were skeptical or dismissive of energy healing. So I connected with like-minded nurses and friends and continued my learning. My thirst for knowledge led me to various courses, books, and seminars. I joined a Holistic Nursing Group and invited remarkable guest speakers from many health disciplines to speak at our monthly meetings. They all presented a new paradigm of health and healing. I had begun my long journey of learning about myriad ways of healing.

This came in tandem with my spiritual growth. It started with a sense of inner peace. I began to understand that my ego was operational for the most part, but that I could also access this peaceful and balanced state within. Both are part of who we are. We are both the physical and the spiritual. I learned how to enter an alpha brain wave state from the deep relaxation exercises I learned in yoga. I also learned to meditate. I joined a Buddhist meditation group for a couple of years. Gaining the discipline to "sit" was part of my training. This was all helpful to my state of being before working on others.

It was also awakening a sense of the mystical in me. I read about the experiences of the saints and mystics. I wondered, "What is enlightenment?" There were so many ideas and practices, and I tried to discover what felt true, for years. A decade ago, my search led to the discovery of the Ascended Masters portal in New Zealand. I felt like I had come home. I finally had a clear direction. This path provided a systematic way to clear all my accumulated karma and raise my spiritual vibration. I am now off the reincarnation wheel and will not return to Earth in a different life.

Being more in harmony and balance has also given me more access to my true guidance, which comes from within—a place from where my intuition rises. I remember feeling like this in the past and then ignoring the feeling in favor of my rational judgment. But if I had gone off course in my life, the next feeling would be regret or dismay due to the fallout from the decision.

Becoming more tuned into my inner guidance has also been great practice for learning how to communicate with my Higher Self. His messages come in different ways, mainly claircognizance. There isn't dialogue with me...at least not yet. He has spoken to me through the lovely and clear channel - Lori Diebold (Chapter Eight). There are interesting ways he gets my attention. Sometimes with humor!

Connecting With My Higher Self

After clearing all karma, I began to learn about my Higher Self. Our Higher Selves become more knowable by showing us their colors and purpose. I know mine as "my Higher Self" or "Edward," and he is a fifth ray master. The fifth ray is the ray of healing, teaching, and truth. His colors are sage green with purple and green overlays leading to a purple edge. A small layer of vibrant, iridescent orange/bronze is around the purple. He is a serious Master but also has a light sense of humor. He helps us to find our voice and speak our truth. You can call on him to help you when you have trouble communicating and need help with the words and the way. He appears in the mind's eye as a man with dark blond hair in tight ringlet curls. His eyes are green, and his nose has a "ski slope." He may present in a brown linen suit, a black tee shirt underneath, and sneakers. Or he may present in his auric colors of sage, purple, and iridescent orange/bronze. He loves me and all humanity so much. His guidance gives direction and a higher purpose to my life. He is always part of my work.

Ascension Dowsing—How It All Started

I became excited about the ancient art of dowsing about thirteen years ago. I saw how wonderful positive effects could occur within a person's home once dowsed. I knew this because I had my house dowsed when my daughter was having nightmares. It turns out there was a negative vortex under the head of her bed and a negative portal in a mirror facing her bed. The dowser "cured" these "hidden things." Without any other intervention, my daughter's nightmares ceased overnight. I decided to learn more about what had occurred.

Jan Thompson and I completed the dowsing program together. We had separate practices for a few years but decided to join forces over five years ago. We find that we each contribute uniquely to the dowsing process. When we started working together, we used the system we had learned. This dowsing system involved using copper rods known as "cures." It was sometimes challenging to place the cures in the ideal location. Once placed, they were also subject to the risk of being moved accidentally.

The idea of the octahedron came over time, and we decided to see how it might work in our home dowsing. We decided to create an etheric octahedron around the home and property through intention. So instead of laying cures strategically around the home and property, we set crystals in the ground at the four compass points of north, south, east, and west. Then through intention, we anchored the middle base of this etheric octahedron. We also connected the top and bottom points of the octahedron to the base through intention. We found that the octahedron we set automatically corrected all the "hidden things" we detected. And we could also discern much bigger upgrades to the overall energy of the home and property. This was an exciting discovery for us! Our new system worked, but we found that sometimes it was challenging to find a good spot to place the crystals. Pavement or concrete walkways got in the way. So instead we started drawing the sacred geometry over a house and property plan using a compass and a ruler. This added a new precision to our work. There were no more obvious physical blocks to overcome on-site. The measurements were consistent. The clearing worked every time.

We gradually refined this new system of dowsing with the help of the Ascended Master St. Germain. This powerful new system uses the sacred geometry of the octahedron and the circle to clear and protect one's environment. It also raises the vibration there to a very high and supportive level. The octahedron has the natural properties of creating balance and harmony. The circle represents unity. We learned how to connect this geometry to the crystalline core of our Earth and the Great Central Sun. One must always have grounding and connections when working in the cosmos. This keeps the work safe and beyond the grasp of interference from any realm. Our new dowsing system always works to raise the vibration in the home to a high level. It corrects all the negative hidden influences in one go. And the high-energy set is stable.

Because the pandemic limited our on-site access to homes, we began to do this work remotely. We have since dowsed many homes internationally. We have completed our dowsing work for many clients in the USA, Australia, and the UK. Our clients are often very intuitive and report immediate and positive changes. We have repeat clients. They see the positive effects of the dowsing and trust the work. The clearing work and use of sacred geometry create a wonderful feeling of, "My home is my sanctuary." There is a steady calmness felt within the spaces we clear. It helps people to be at their best. The new high vibration created is very supportive of anyone living there.

What is the Work of Dowsing?

Dowsing rods are the tools we use to detect various "hidden things" that can lower the energy in one's home. There are many types of "hidden things." These can negatively impact the home and the people living there. We normally find the overall energy readings to be below ten. Through our work, we can raise the energy levels much, much higher.

We often find entities such as discarnate spirits (AKA ghosts!). Ghosts are earth-bound discarnate spirits. Their human host may have had a sudden or traumatic death, and they remain on Earth without knowing where to go. They missed the window of opportunity to go to the light when their human host passed. They are in between realms. They often stay close to the area that is familiar to them. They sometimes attach to others but generally do not mean to harm.

But other types of entities also exist, and these like to interfere with humans. They can attach to us and cause illness or misdirection. This type can move in and out of the lower fourth dimension to Earth via negative portals. A negative portal allows them to travel between their plane of existence and ours. Negative portals are often at water drain sites. They can create a strong negative energetic pull downwards. This can lead to sleep issues and can lower immunity. They can also come into the home through antique furniture or even mirrors. When we dowse, we first detect if there are any negative portals and close them immediately. We provide the entities with an opening which is a temporary positive portal to return to the love and light of God. We do so with the help of Ascended Masters. We invite them to choose this opportunity. The entities that have more malevolent intentions often resist this. Sometimes we call in Archangel Michael. He gets the job done! They always return to the light because it is very hard to resist. It is very humbling to observe. This is an important and benevolent aspect of the service we provide. There is a link to everything in the cosmos. We stay unharmed by establishing these connections. It is so important in our work. There are many false "pretenders." We safely avoid them and their potential to create harm.

Other "hidden things" are negative vortexes. These are disturbances in the ley lines that run north and south as well as east and west around the earth. They are magnetic fields. These lines are invisible, like our latitude, longitude, and prime meridian. (Maritime navigation is reliant on these invisible lines). The ley lines can become misaligned due to geophysical events like earthquakes and human activities. This can create a downward-pulling energy called a negative vortex in the related area. Disturbed sleep and nightmares are common for people sleeping over a negative vortex. These locations are often intuitively avoided by the people in the house. It doesn't feel good to spend time in these areas. The opposite is true of a positive vortex. These are lovely finds in a home. This may be a favorite place to sit.

We look for geopathic stress lines because they can create illness if too many converge in one spot. They usually come from fault lines and water lines underground. Even very deep underground water can affect the home.

EMF (electromagnetic frequency) and radio frequencies generally negatively impact the home or property. EMF and radio frequency lines come from power boxes and poles, cell towers outside the home, or a smart meter. They also come from microwaves, cell phones, televisions, and computers within the home. Even electrical outlets are a source of EMF. All these lines can impact our energy and our health. We often find areas that are very low in energy in the home. This can result from the confluence of several lines converging in an area. The sacred geometry automatically corrects these issues every time.

This work is very effective. People often report that they knew when we had completed the dowsing. Their homes or spaces felt clean, clear, and peaceful. Our clients are often very intuitive and report immediate and positive changes.

There have been many times we made discoveries as we dowsed a property. For instance, we now create a violet flame "firewall" around the client's property. This is general protection against unseen breaches by hackers. Everyone uses the world wide web now. We are all at some risk of interference with our information systems. The etheric "firewall" we create is extra protection.

We are continually learning and growing in the art of Ascension Dowsing. We know that the high vibration created each time is stable. It stays within the etheric structures we have drawn and programmed. We program the octahedrons with certain intentions for protection. We find this process has integrity and lasts. When we checked homes we dowsed two years ago, we found the sacred geometry intact. The energy remains at a high level, and the protection is holding.

Our reports show the clients where the octahedron's center point or "Now" point is. This is a place of higher vibration. Being in this spot, one can sometimes feel a still point. This is where you can stand and state intentions for your highest good. You can more easily draw your intentions into manifestation. In this spot, you can express your dreams for your highest good through affirmations and intentions about health, happiness, relationships, abundance, satisfying work or service, etc.

We create a high vibration in your home. This state provides ongoing support for the people living there. Your home becomes a welcome retreat from the impact of the energies we interact with daily. The energy is refreshing, healing, supportive, and enriching.

There is so much permanent value in this work. This is so important in these times of ascension. We need support during the major changes our world is going through now. We can all use a safe place, a sanctuary; somewhere we can thrive.

Success Stories for our Clients with Ascension Dowsing

There are three stories in this section. They all show how immediate and profound the changes are once we complete dowsing. I will also describe how validating this work has been for the clients who sought our assistance. You will read about certain discoveries we found and corrected in these stories. You will read about how we cleared entities, closed negative portals, and changed negative vortexes. You will see how the sacred geometry prevents impact from electromagnetic frequencies and geopathic stress. You will also see how clients use the still point created within the sacred geometry.

A Ghost Story

The first story is from a woman who works with angels and Ascended Masters. Her practice is "Soul Inspired Animal Communication," and she also provides "Angel Empowerment" sessions. She is an intuitive/empath who is very sensitive to the presence of out-of-body entities.

Anna asked us to dowse her home and property because she often saw disembodied spirits (ghosts) floating through her home. She spent countless hours each week, including daily work, to keep her home clear and clean. She works out of her home and didn't want interference and interruption in her work. These ghosts were disturbing, and she wanted a permanent solution. We found one negative portal in the mechanical room, which we closed. We checked for and detected the presence of some entities. We released the spirits in Anna's home first, and then Jan and I completed the dowsing. We set up an etheric barrier through intention. This was to prevent disembodied spirits from entering Anna's home.

Anna told us later that she knew when we had completed the work. She woke up the next day and felt a big difference in her home. It felt clean and clear to her. She found our dowsing report when she checked her email the next morning. She realized that the work had been completed the prior evening. The spirits were gone, and she has never been bothered by the presence of any since! Anna is so delighted. She is relieved to be free and clear of these bothersome beings, and she loves her home's high vibe. She now enjoys working out of her home office. She finds that she has gained new confidence in her work. No longer are spirits travelling through her home. She says the energy in her home is now lighter and more fluid. She also finds the places where she places her crystals have a higher vibration. She is very confident in the protection of the octahedron. She has told all her spirit-minded friends they must have us dowse their homes and places they work in. Anna is a very satisfied customer. And it thrilled us to see this work's positive and permanent outcome!

Joanne's Classroom and Apartment

Joanne asked if we could clear and protect her classroom within her school. Joanne is a very intuitive/perceptive person. She can sense the presence of entities, cords, and other attachments in her students. She wanted to create a clean energy environment in her classroom that would support her work. My partner Jan dowses her own daughter's classroom every September. So we knew dowsing one classroom within the whole school was doable.

Joanne knew when we had completed our work. She felt that still point in the center of her classroom immediately. When the vice principal stood in the center point of the octahedron, she said that the space felt quiet. Joanne says that her classroom is often visited by other teachers who enjoy being in this space. Sometimes they come by to do some healing work with her. Joanne is now enjoying the clean and clear space. It is now free of entities and negative energies that interfered with her and her students. These things were an energy drain. She often works with students needing conflict management and/or who have other issues. She finds that now in the classroom, they are clear thinkers who can get the bigger picture. They feel safe, secure, and free to speak their truth in this environment. She finds they have an enlightened view of what is happening. They can release old ways and return to wholeness where they should be. They are awakening in this new energy. Joanne also finds the new energy highly supportive of her healing work. The effects in her classroom have been "out of this world."

Joanne then asked us to dowse the private living space she rented within a home. Before dowsing, her cat would not walk on the floor. Instead, the cat jumped from couch to chair to counter. Joanne sensed the cat was wary of certain spots in the apartment. When we completed the dowsing, the cat left its perch and began walking on the floor. Joanne said she felt the still point and how deeply calming and centering this was for her. Her landlord became friendlier and easier to get along with. Whereas before, she would find him quite negative; since the dowsing, he is much more positive. Before the dowsing, he was all "doom and gloom." That energy is all gone now. She finds the energy of her place amazing. Joanne has also found her twin flame and is now married to him. They are both on a dedicated spiritual path.

Joanne also recommends our work as an essential "must-do" to her friends. Ascension Dowsing is just one of those things that may need to be experienced to be believed. Each person will have standard as well as unique experiences with it. But they will all be transformative!

All Jammed Up

Jan and I detected that this house had a sense of seizing up, as if it had experienced some kind of shock. Something big had affected the house. Jan sensed it came diagonally from across the street. Andrea confirmed a gas explosion occurred in the house across the street a few years prior. She was standing in her living room at the time of the explosion. She heard the living room window shatter. She realized that flying shards of glass could have cut into her. Fortunately, a film on the windows contained any of those shards of broken glass.

We found the overall energy in the house was around two, which is very low. Andrea described feeling low in energy while in the house. She also reported that there was a part of the basement where the energy didn't feel good. She used that space to store unused furniture, boxes, and bins. We measured that energy as a minus three, which is unhealthy. This was the location of a negative vortex. There were five negative vortexes on the property. We cleared all of them through our dowsing. Ley lines are naturally occurring etheric lines around the earth. They run north and south as well as east and west and are magnetic in origin. When the ley lines are in a 90-degree alignment, they form positive energy spots. These are called positive vortexes. We often find positive vortexes in homes and on properties. These are lovely spots to sit or meditate in. Negative vortexes are created from the misalignment of the ley lines. This can decrease one's energy, create sleep issues, and lead to health concerns. In the floors above a negative or positive vortex, there will be a doubling and tripling effect of the vortex. This magnifies the effect of the vortex. In this case, Andrea's husband, Joe, had his office directly above this basement space. Andrea had her office directly above his. Andrea placed various crystals around her healing room. She also hung pictures of Masters' portals and placed statues of spiritual beings in her room. This brought the energy in her room up somewhat. She had also mitigated the negative effects of the negative vortex in her husband's office. Dowsing either neutralizes all negative vortexes or often changes them into positive vortexes. In this case, the energies shifted dramatically to the positive in the house after we completed the dowsing. Andrea said the house felt like it loosened up some of that stuck energy and relaxed. She no longer had to work to mitigate the negative energy on the floors above the basement. She was in awe of the new energy all through the house. After the dowsing, she could immediately feel the newly raised vibration's intensity. Being a highly sensitive intuitive, it took her two full days to integrate. She now felt so much happier in her home. Things had changed. Before the dowsing she felt low in energy while in her house. Andrea is a very positive, light-hearted human who thrives in her home's new energy.

She can now stand in her kitchen at the center point of the octahedron and clear anything attached to her aura that she may have picked up unintentionally during the day. She also reported that when her son Adam was home recently on a visit from college, he didn't bother to play with his video games in the basement. This had previously been his passion. She was surprised and pleased with this unexpected outcome for her son. She enjoyed his visit more than usual at that time. She also noted that he was able to sleep well after the dowsing. This was great because he has had chronic sleep issues. Another positive outcome is for her friend Chloe, who works out of Andrea's home once a month. Chloe reports her work has moved to a new level since the dowsing. Sometimes we hear from the client about unanticipated positive outcomes from our dowsing. These are lovely surprises and always make us grateful for our work. Andrea continues to enjoy the high vibes in her home and tells all her like-minded friends to contact us!

When we set an octahedron around a property, we create a stable conduit between the cosmos and the earth's crystalline core. A high vibration within it can feel like a wonderful sanctuary in which to live. For anyone on an active path of ascension, this energetic support set up with our dowsing can be profound. The potential is there for powerful benefits for anyone once your home is dowsed.

To read more about us and our work and to discover what else we can do through our dowsing, go to our website at www.ascension-dowsing.com.

Modern Ascension

In the fall of 2018, I was guided to create a book with many others about the unique and novel Ascension path that we are on. We each wrote about our lives and spiritual paths and the enormous challenges faced by some. The book's title is *Modern Ascension.* It is about awakening to the truth of our being...that we are spiritual beings having a human experience. And the life we are experiencing now is but one of many that our soul has lived embodied over time. The thirteen stories in this book are from individuals who followed a new spiritual initiates' path. One that put us all on the rapid path of ascension. The stories are all so varied. We all come from different cultures and have unique life experiences. Some of the stories reflect extraordinary hardship. The path of Ascension is very trying, yet it has many highlights along the way and is so worth the adventure. Ascension is the higher purpose of our existence. We come into this life veiled to knowing we are here to clear our karma and raise our vibration. Once we wake up to this truth, we can do this work. This is Ascension. We can do this within the context of ordinary life. We each have something unique to offer in our roles as humans. Yet the spiritual purpose of our existence is to clear all karma and raise our vibration. Once we clear our karma, we are no longer bound to the Earth and its human cycles of reincarnation. There is no need to return for more lifetimes of trauma and drama. Thus completing our earthly journey. The soul is then taken into the vast Higher Self. The Higher Self no longer needs to create more human lives to work towards this plan. And once this human life is complete, the Higher Self is no longer tied to the Earth plane. They have graduated and will continue their Ascension journey as we will ours.

This initiation path has multiple steps, each building on the other. You can't buy it. You can't skip any steps. You must walk the path as a conscious and wise being, learning how to become an agent of love in this life. You learn to recognize we are all divine aspects of the one Source/God. Our Higher Selves love us wholly. They work through us to achieve their intentions of helping humanity. They are so proud of us and how far we have come as partners on this Ascension path with them. It is an endless journey home. The purpose of this book is to stimulate awakening. And to encourage those already seeking to find a clear Ascension path. My Higher Self says that the words in the book, *Modern Ascension,* are healing words.

Carol Anne Halstead, Canada

Website: www.ascensiondowsing.com

Facebook: https://www.facebook.com/ascensiondowsing

Chapter Five

A Lotus in Troubled Soil: Reconnecting to Joy Within

by Joy Vottus

Changing your life begins by consciously making different choices in alignment with your soul's true desires.

-Joy Vottus

Formative Years

I was born in Taipei, Taiwan, in the 1970s, the eldest of three sisters. I lived in a large extended family unit, with my parents, grandparents, uncle, and aunty. I was a sensitive and serious child. My experience of family life was made complex by my father not having a consistent job and my mother being the responsible person in the family. She worked hard to keep the family together. My attitude to life was strongly influenced by seeing my mother's responsible and hard-working approach to life. This was something that influenced my choices as I grew to become an adult and find my way in life. From an early age, I recognised the importance of personal discipline and focus, and saw how my mother fought hard to make our lives successful.

Taiwanese culture is centred around patriarchal concepts. So when I was born, my mother had considerable disappointment that I was a girl. She had hoped for a boy to carry forward the bloodline and legacy of the family. Having a boy in Chinese culture is something families always aim for. Whereas boys are a source of pride, girls have always occupied a much lower status in society, and therefore baby girls are less welcome. So despite my sensitivity—being born as an empath—I felt considerable pressure to be more like a boy than a girl. Consequently, I would wear trousers rather than the skirts and dresses that other girls my age wore. The feminine side of me, I feel, was suppressed from my early childhood. I had a sense of difference from an early age, not simply from feeling my mother's disappointment with my gender, but also because I discovered quickly that I had spiritual gifts that others did not.

From age five, I spent much of my time with my grandmother, who practised a belief system called Yiguandao. It is a religious sect that combines Taoism, Buddhism, Confucianism, and even the salvationist elements of religions like Christianity. As I became attuned to my higher awareness and spiritual gifts during my time with her, I discovered that just as I could tune in to people and feel their emotions directly, I could also tune in to the spirit world and other dimensions. This experience was dramatic and quite alarming for me and my parents. I would hear voices, feel the presence of beings, and feel trapped when in bed, unable to escape the influence of dark presences from another realm of existence, and even unable to awake. I sometimes lived a nightmare of being trapped by entities that frightened me.

My parents were worried about me, so they took me to see a psychic medium to help close down some of my psychic abilities. To some extent this succeeded, but in my early teen years I would again experience a form of spirit control where I would feel my body was possessed in my sleep, and I would have no control over my nervous system. During this period I developed a strong ability to feel others' feelings and hidden intentions and to be very aware of energetic processes beyond normal perceptual comprehension.

As I left childhood, I threw my energies into schoolwork, which was a very strict regime in Taiwan. I found my focus in life, as I worked on qualifying and becoming ready to enter the world of adulthood and material responsibility. My sensitivity and energetic awareness as an empath remained, but I became ever more sucked into the expectations of life. I felt encouraged and even pressured to study, work, and fulfill myself with a career and, one day, my own family.

I graduated from university in 1995 with a Bachelor of Arts, majoring in English, and met my husband the same year. My focus was on external life, including jobs ranging from secretary and admin to English teaching. It meant that my inner world and spiritual interests faded into the background. My awareness of other dimensions and a greater spiritual reality was repressed as I proceeded to conform to expectations. I began to live a conventional life focussed on material comfort and family, like everyone I knew, culminating in the birth of my son in my late twenties, and a newfound role in life as a mum. I enjoyed my work and found motherhood fulfilling, but as time went on I was in my thirties, and the sensitive side of myself, the part of me that had always been spiritually aware and that I had repressed to fit in with others' expectations, began to resurface.

Tibetan Buddhist Practices

In my mid-thirties, I rediscovered my spirituality and began to explore it within Tibetan Buddhism. I was fascinated by the many miracles associated with Tibetan monks' spiritual practices and recitation of mantras. I felt drawn to the religion, partly because I was primed for the interest of my grandmother's practices that she had introduced me to as a child. I was already familiar with many of the concepts and strongly drawn to the liberation from the endless cycle of death and rebirth. My grandmother's Yiguandao practice was founded on the belief in "Chiuan Sanbo," or the "Offering of the three treasures" which are the *xuanguan* (the heavenly portal), the *koujue* (a mantra), and *hetong* (the hand gesture). With this "Chiuan Sanbo" initiation, the Yiguandao members believe that they transcend the cycle of life and death to ascend directly to heaven when they die.

In the early days of my practices of Tibetan Buddhism, I dreamed that I met Maitreya Buddha. He is believed to be the future Buddha who will come to reinstate the dharma, or way of right action. In the dream I was shown a purple lotus, which is a Buddhist symbol of spiritual awakening and the development of spiritual wisdom. I felt that I was on the right path and was being given a sign to continue on the path to self-realisation. During this period, I also reconnected more strongly with my empath energy and my ability to feel multiple levels of other people's emotional states. One of my fellow students introduced me to Reiki and energy healing as a whole, which strongly resonated with me. It felt like a doorway, a portal, had opened in my life to re-inhabit my spiritual self without the fear and anxiety I had had as a child; a whole new avenue of personal development was opening up for me.

From 2009 to 2012, I undertook intensive work in Tibetan Buddhism and practised strongly. Yet after a few years, I felt myself becoming impatient. My restless fire sign Sagittarius nature wanted to see results that were very slow to transpire, and I felt frustrated that my work was yielding such slow progress. I felt there must be a way to develop myself in a more direct and dynamic way. I began to look around for something that would galvanise my spiritual abilities and propel me forward. It felt so hard that I had found my path again after being asleep spiritually for so long. My spiritual self is in the process, yet I could not break through barriers that held me back in my growth.

New Age Traps

In 2012, at a spiritual workshop I attended, I had my first kundalini activation. I had developed a renewed interest in all things spiritual because of the 2012 doomsday scenario of the Mayan Calendar, which I am now embarrassed to admit. This experience of kundalini activation was the major turning point for me to understand where and how I was to move forward in my spiritual work. I saw clearly that I was being drawn to do energy work as a focus on my spiritual path.

At this time, I met members of a spiritual group at a stand at a Mind Body and Spirit festival. I became convinced that the group seemed to offer all I was looking for in my spiritual development. I was soon involved heavily as a volunteer and became one of the most devoted disciples. After initially feeling elevated spiritually through my experiences in the group, what transpired was a period of five years of systematic exploitation and manipulation. From 2012 to 2017, I worked with this group and came to believe that the total control and hierarchical behaviour that I was experiencing was all for my own benefit. I chose to give my power away and innocently believed that the "guru" couple I followed could eventually lead me to soul liberation. Along with the other members of what I later understood had been a cult, I was routinely subjected to a regime of four hours of sleep a night before being given long and time-consuming menial tasks. These tasks were always subject to criticisms or deliberately manufactured failures where it was impossible to succeed, and always an opportunity for condescending and vicious lectures and ritual humiliation.

Eventually, like many others, I was also subjected to long hours of public confessionals, where the cult leaders and the other core disciples verbally threatened and humiliated me. I was forced to say awful things about myself to give them enough "evidence" that could incriminate me, a "coming clean" practice that was routine and regarded as of prime benefit for soul evolution in the group. After about four months of intensive and long sessions of mental and psychological abuse, I would no longer know who I was. I felt very lost and scattered, even wishing to die rather than experience the torment of being brutally criticised and humiliated by people who I innocently loved, trusted, and respected.

In pursuit of a spiritual awakening, I had found myself within a group that, rather than elevate the consciousness and activate the ascension of its members, actively sought to wield power and control over their lives, their minds, and even their finances. It took five years to come to the realisation that the group was not genuine; what I was learning was nothing but a false belief system. I was actually being taught to accept others' power and authority over me with blind trust, and rather than help me spiritually evolve, the group was isolating me from my own family. Their agenda of trying to separate me from my family, and even send representatives to run me down to them at my home, was the final straw, and I decided to leave the group. I had learned a valuable lesson that my self-worth was more than allowing others to tell me who I was. I recognised, in a moment of clarity, that my relationship with my spiritual self could not be controlled by others.

Rising from the Ashes

I left the group mentally, emotionally, and spiritually traumatised, and went through a period of depression. For a few months I lost all hope, and all the confidence I had ever had. I really thought it was the end of me; I was broken and scattered. But deep inside me, I knew I couldn't continue to live like this and allow myself to be defeated by those people trying to subjugate my will. After a few months of contemplation, I decided to pick myself up, with the limited resources I could find, to start my healing process. I was trying to re-centre myself through forgiveness, including self-forgiveness, letting go, and releasing the pain. This healing process helped me to look back and see my journey.

From childhood, I lacked self-belief yet connected deeply to my innate spiritual gifts. I had discovered that despite feeling I did not fit in in society and was unhappy with where I was in my personal identity, I had even greater differences through my spiritual awareness and enhanced empathic traits. I had suppressed these traits and abilities after some early traumatic experiences with spirit entities and beings that frightened me as a sensitive and vulnerable child. I had carried this awareness with me, buried but always present, and always a thorn in my side in later years, manifesting as a feeling of not being truly authentic and in tune with myself.

As I developed as a child, I switched my focus away from my differences with others, away from a journey of self-exploration and self-acceptance. Instead I chose to conform, to live a life occupied with chasing mundane goals of material security, conforming to others' expectations, and having a family, which was nevertheless a joyful experience. However, I always felt that a part of me was not truly being allowed room to breathe and express itself. My spirit had been stifled by not exploring my true nature, and by avoiding confronting my blockages.

While Tibetan Buddhism had inspired me to recommence the journey within, it had frustrated me in its inability to help me rapidly push through my blocks, and so I had become attracted to energy work. After exploring energy work and renewing my passion for spiritual work, I had accepted—without discrimination—the wild claims of the soul origins and spiritual gifts of the cult leaders I then followed for several years. Looking back, spending several painful years with a cult taught me that I could no longer give my power to others, but that my spiritual awareness was enough to guide me to greater spiritual growth. I recognised that not only is my self-worth to be found within myself, my own beauty self-flowering and not created by others, but that wisdom is within and cannot be supplied by another. That any help received from others is only a stimulus for one's own inner mastery to be awakened.

Despite my difficult journeys in the spiritual field, always looking outward to external agencies for answers, two years later I was led, happily, to a genuine spiritual group that honours my inner work. This authentic group recognizes the sovereignty of each being's path on the spiritual journey of Ascension from the cycle of karma and death/rebirth. And in turn I have come full circle. In a sense, I have returned to my grandmother's spiritual beliefs, the possibility of spiritual Ascension through my own efforts, not through hope and belief in external agents. Through my own intelligently directed spiritual efforts, surrendering what is not self, what is no longer my path, what no longer is a story I need to hold onto in my life, I am evolving.

Higher Self Embodiment and Synchronicities

I started to work with the Masters in the Ascension Portal located in New Zealand in early 2020, whose energy work and teachings have helped me make a quantum leap in my spiritual growth and transformation. I immediately dedicated myself to my Ascension path, with many energy-clearing sessions that helped to release the dross and karma stored in the chakra systems. This ultimately enabled me to embody 100 percent of light in my chakra system. As a result, my kundalini is now fully awakened, and my upper chakras from the eighth to the twelfth are activated. All this background work has made it possible for me to embark on the process of embodying my Higher Self in this physical existence. This enables me to be a pure channel to deliver the highest and purest form of energy for my services.

My Higher Self is the Alpha (Divine Masculine) aspect of the sixth ray, the ray of the goddess and the ray of devotion. At the beginning of the embodiment process, I saw a golden ring embedded with diamond-like golden-white light through the third eye. A few days later, I had this epiphany that it was an "engagement" sign (shown as an engagement ring) from my Higher Self anchored in my Holy Heart, and the sparks of lights on the ring are the indication that the Higher Self's light has "embedded" in me.

A few months later, my Higher Self's name came to me as "Vottus" when I connected to Him in the Holy Heart. I had no knowledge about this word until I searched on the Internet. It originated from the Latin "Vōtus," which is a masculine word meaning "promised," "vowed," or "devoted to." In addition, there are six characters in total (synchronicity of the sixth Ray). For me, it's a triple confirmation that Vottus is the name of my Higher Self. His aura is purple with warmth and loving energy. I can feel His powerful presence when I consciously connect to Him. He often gives me signs, support, and guidance in many ways. Seeing repeating numbers in meaningful synchronicities has become the norm of my daily life.

Just as I discovered my Higher Self's name, I wondered if there was a way to have an energy drawing of him. One month later, Tamara, a higher Initiate, approached me and told me she had made a painting for me. When I saw the painting, straight away I recognized it was my Higher Self's energy—the purple and gold colours are the sixth ray elements, my Higher Self also has the same blue in His energy signature as in the painting. In the centre, there is a diamond-shaped frame in brown, it looks like the initial "V" for Vottus in the bottom part; on the top of the diamond shape are six curves, another synchronicity of the sixth ray.

I had never mentioned anything about my Higher Self to Tamara before. She told me it was her most recent work guided by her Higher Self. After having some conversations with her, I realised that it was our Higher Self connection that had produced this painting using her talents. Apparently my Higher Self heard me and blessed me with this precious gift as a surprise, and a few weeks later the parcel arrived exactly on my birthday! After tuning in with my Higher Self, I got the message that this was my Higher Self's fifth dimension energy portal, a gateway to His energy field, to other dimensions of His existence. It's connected to my Holy Heart and the eighth chakra; I recognised that I could connect to this portal for healing and receiving guidance from my Higher Self. It is indeed a sacred space for me and my Higher Self. These are just some of the examples of amazing synchronicities I have experienced, and sometimes I am just in awe of how things are orchestrated, and manifesting miracles in my day-to-day life.

Twin Flame Journey and the Clearing of Past Lives

My Higher Self knows very well when to give me a nudge to tell me how to move on in every step of my personal transformation. Not too long after passing the 30 percent of Higher Self embodiment, my twin flame suddenly showed up unexpectedly. Initially I was very excited to discover a connection with my twin flame in this physical reality. I made completely sure by verifying it through Astrology, an Akashic Record reading, and through the energy connection itself. However, I was soon to be painfully disillusioned, as the runner and chaser archetypal dynamic played out within just one week.

The polarity of the twin flame energy triggered a huge feeling of rejection for me. I felt a lot of pain and began working on clearing the energy blocks that were causing the separation on the three-D level. Through navigating the karmic patterns and energies, many past-live wounds and traumas were revealed, to be released, transmuted, and healed. This caused me to go through deeper levels of purging so that I could be in alignment with the Divine path planned by my Higher Self.

In the past I had been focusing on the "vertical Ascension," which is to deepen the connection with my Divine Self, the Creator, the Source. Other Divine Connections are equally important—my Higher Self guided me to work, through the twin flame connection, on the embodiment of balanced Divine Feminine and Masculine Selves. We all have feminine and masculine aspects within us. Although our Higher Self can be Alpha (Divine Masculine) or Omega (Divine Feminine), the Masculine and Feminine are always balanced regardless of whether they present themselves as Alpha or Omega. The imbalance of feminine and masculine energies within the individual can also affect the twin flame relationship.

While working on clearing the karmic patterns and energies from my twin flame connection, a few significant past lifetimes were revealed to me. Out of my 13,546 incarnations, I could be a "nobody" or a "somebody." After all, as a soul having human experiences, it is not surprising that I have played different roles throughout these lifetimes to experience three-D reality and learn a diverse variety of life lessons. Some of the lifetimes that were revealed to me were historical public figures, so I would read their stories and relate the connection with the twin flame or myself in that particular lifetime. Often the lifetimes of these historical public figures could be intense and need massive clearing. Just like clearing, any karmic issues were pulled out for a clearing, along with all the trauma, belief systems, patterns, programs, energy cords, imprints, cellular memories, and ancestral lines from the original lifetime, and on through the subsequent lifetimes, dimensions, and timelines!

After nine months of exhaustive energy work, it finally called a halt to the work on my twin flame connection, and I felt a great sense of relief. It was not an easy process as I needed to constantly go through and experience the wounds and pains of lifetimes of connections. The profound realisation I had is that we can always connect to our twin flame through our Higher Self connection to them, purely on the energetic level. It is not always necessary to have physical encounters, if the twin flame is not ready yet, or it's not in the Higher Self's Divine plan. Walking this journey has helped me dive deeper into the dynamics of the twin flame connection and cleared out the energy entanglements from more than four hundred past lifetimes. It has been a rare, once in many lifetimes, opportunity for me to go through such deep levels of clearing, to forgive and let go. As a result of the inner work during my twin flame journey, I have been energetically prepared to attract the ideal soulmate I have been looking for.

During the process, I was given a nudge by my Higher Self to contact Tamara to draw a couple of paintings of the Twin Flame portal for me. I was also guided by my Higher Self to offer twin flame/soulmate Akashic records readings to assist people in finding and exploring the past and present lifetimes' connections, as well as the Soul-level blocks and associated restrictions. By offering personalised clearing and healing, I aim to help people progress in their twin flame/soulmate relationships. My Higher Self has been preparing me to assist people walking on this path by working on myself first, and despite how painful the process was, I am grateful for the lessons I have received along the way!

For more information about Twin Flame/Soulmate Reading and Clearing:

https://www.awakeningwithjoy.com/product-page/twinflame-soulmate-relationship-reading

Akashic Record Reading & Clearing

Despite the ups and downs, I have diligently worked on myself over the past fifteen years, eventually strengthening the connection to my true essence. This has been not only my Higher Self, but also the connection with the Source/Divine Creator as an awakened Soul. It's my greatest passion to support people who are on their awakening and Ascension journey.

I have successfully developed my ability to channel and embody high-vibration pure energy to facilitate the healing process through modalities such as Quantum Touch, Access Bars, Soul Realignment Akashic Record Reading, etc. The facility to use these modalities is more than simply knowing the techniques, but also knowing and accessing my multidimensionality, and thus my innate abilities as an intuitive healer and reader. I have been guided by my Higher Self to work with Ascended Masters, Cosmic Masters, Archangels, and light beings to assist clients in raising their light quotient, and to facilitate their personal transformation and Soul evolution.

I have come across many people who would like to work on themselves but have little clue where to start. I often recommend people start with the Soul Realignment Akashic Record reading and clearing as a starting point for personal development and transformation. The Akashic record reading is a structured reading. It helps to navigate the Soul's origination, Soul vibration rate, Divine gift, Soul's unique specialisation, primary life lesson, chakra leakages, attached Souls, and karmic patterns. It also works with negative portals or astral travel that are holding one back, as well as soul vows and contracts that can keep us bound to a lower energetic matrix.

The reading helps my clients better understand why they are who they are, and through the energy work I help them align with their Divine Soul Blueprint to move forward in their lives. After the reading, I work with my Higher Self and Ascended Masters to clear out any blocks and restrictions, karmic patterns, and anything else that had been picked up from the Akashic Record reading. This opens the door for more in-depth clearing and healing, as I have found that once the client starts their healing process, the issues will then present themselves spontaneously for further clearing and healing.

One of my clients, Arakah, started to consult me on the challenges in her life, such as getting a driver's licence; having failed the test many times in the past. She also needed to understand how to transcend the stress she was experiencing while studying for her occupational therapy qualification. I went through her Akashic Records to find the root causes of her difficulties and did multidimensional clearing and healing for her. I also helped her to reconnect with the skills and knowledge she had developed from certain past lifetimes, and to re-empower herself. I received guidance from my Higher Self and offered assistance for her to move forward constructively, empowered and with optimism. After one and a half years working with me, she is now a qualified occupational therapist and has found a position that has a positive and pleasant working environment. This is her testimonial from my work:

> *Joy has been an incredible healer for me. I have been engaging her regularly to help me in all aspects of my life since October 2021. Her powerful energy work has shifted so much of my energy and helped me overcome numerous challenges and obstacles! Most importantly, through her effective energy work, Joy has helped me achieve what I thought was impossible. For the past twenty years, I have sought many healers to help me clear my issues, shift my perspective, and transform myself. But Joy is the only healer I continue to see so regularly & consistently. She has helped me in so many aspects of my life: my health, my studies,*

my relationship with my partner, my work, and even helped me get my driving licence. I will elaborate on each of them respectively.

First of all, Joy's energy work has allowed me to maintain good health. Due to stress from work and studies, I often have very bad migraines and also am unable to sleep well at night. Through many layers of deep cleansing, my severe migraine was eased, and I am now enjoying a better quality of sleep. In addition, she helped me clear the coronavirus vaccine. I needed to take two doses of vaccinations to keep my job, but I was very worried about the side effects of the vaccinations. But after Joy helped me clear out the vaccinations energetically, I experienced no side effects from it apart from a sore arm. Moreover, Joy has also helped me strengthen my immune system and respiration system. I did not fall sick at all in the one year of seeing her (From October 2021 to October 2022).

Secondly, I was doing a thesis for my Honours for the whole of last year. I had issues such as believing I am not good enough, unhealthy self-judgement, childhood trauma of being badly criticised by family and former schoolteachers, etc, which hindered me from doing my thesis well. Joy helped me clear the issue one by one every time I saw her! In mid-December last year, I received the great news that I achieved first-class Honours for my thesis :)

Thirdly, through a relationship reading, Joy identified the key issues causing problems between my partner and me. A few months ago, my partner and I had a severe conflict, and I desperately sought help from

Joy. Just two days after Joy cleared those key issues, my partner and I were able to communicate with each other calmly and resolve our conflicts:)

Fourthly, in order to get my licence to practise occupational therapy, I need to get 65 percent for four components of an English test. After the first attempt at the test, I got below sixty-five marks and felt devastated. Joy went the extra mile to coach and guide me through the steps that would help me get through this test along with her powerful energy work. I got the marks I needed to get my Occupational Therapist's License on my second attempt at the English Test! I am now working very happily as an Occupational Therapist in a paediatric clinic :)

Last but not least, Joy created another miracle for me—I got my driving licence on my first test attempt in an area with busy traffic in Melbourne. About twelve years ago, I failed my driving test three times in Singapore. From then on, I believed that I would never be able to drive, and I would never be competent in driving. This belief was a huge obstacle for me! Fortunately, Joy supported me in clearing this huge obstacle! I have my own car now and have been driving for the past seven months. Driving is something I never thought was going to be possible for me! But Joy made it happen for me!

My most sincere gratitude to Joy! Not only did I have the honour to receive healing from such a dedicated and powerful healer, but I also found and made a great friend who I can trust and deeply connect with for the rest of my life :)

For more information about Soul Realignment Reading:

https://www.awakeningwithjoy.com/product-page/soul-realignment-reading

For more information about Multi-dimensional Clearing & Healing:

https://www.awakeningwithjoy.com/product-page/multidimensional-clearing-healing

Relationship Readings and Clearings

Lyn is another client who approached me for an Akashic Records reading initially. These readings often bring up relationship issues for clearing and healing, and often there is not simply an issue with romantic relationships but also some complex family issues. Issues in relationships often stem back to dynamics from childhood. I did a relationship reading with her to navigate the karmic energies shared with her partner, including karmic patterns, blocks and restrictions, and the life lessons for their relationship. Lyn is one of many clients who I have worked with on relationship dynamics who has gone through many positive shifts in their relationships. Here, Lyn from Central Coast Australia describes her experience with me:

> *Over many years, my partner and I have explored the wide spectrum of spiritual modalities with varying results. Joy's Akashic Records Readings provided a profoundly different experience...A totally insightful level of perspective and knowledge that alters your view of who you are and, importantly, what has led you to this state of being. We agreed that we would (individually or together) never have discovered this deep, deep level of understanding. Joy, dare I say it, is a JOY! Professional, Empathetic, and Direct—she*

covers a vast array of specific subjects, relevant to you and your Soul Journey. Information from your past is Transformative. It allows a transitional process to integrate this new factual data into your current life—with powerful results.

Kate from Melbourne, Australia, was attracted to my 2022.2.22 portal Soul-alignment meditation video recording on my YouTube channel. She felt a major realignment and shift happening after watching the recording. So, like many other clients, she did her Soul Realignment Akashic Records reading and clearings, which was a catalyst for bringing up issues she had with some family members. She felt energetically stuck through complex entanglements with these family members, so we proceeded to examine the energetic dynamic with each person, to work on their relationship reading, gain clarity on the nature of the connection, and locate the root causes of issues. After doing this, we cleared out the cords, threads, and karmic entanglement that were holding back the relationships. After each clearing session, she felt significant shifts and felt greatly relieved, and she always felt lighter after each session.

For more information about Relationship Reading:

https://www.awakeningwithjoy.com/product-page/twinflame-soulmate-relationship-reading

Portal Meditation and Manifestation

As we know, everything is energy, frequency, and vibration. An energy portal is a doorway to access different energies, frequencies, and vibrations, even across different timelines, space, or dimensions. We access different energy portals all the time, knowingly or unknowingly, especially when we sleep. As human beings, we are literally the walking portals of our Souls who are having human experiences.

When we are consciously walking the spiritual awakening path or Ascension journey, there are more opportunities to expose ourselves to many different types of portals within our energy system (such as chakras) or outside our energy system (such as astral travel). The chakras are our internal energy portals we often access, especially when we meditate or do energy work.

Other than these portals mentioned, we are also exposed to the planetary portal energies, such as Solar/Lunar Eclipse, New Moon, Full Moon, Solstice/Equinox, or numerological portal days, etc. all the time. There are organic and positive portal energies that help to accelerate our Soul evolution, yet there are also other astral energies coming through these portals that can have a damaging effect if people don't anchor their energies properly.

I am passionate about offering portal meditation to bring through pure portal energy in combination with different energy themes. Sometimes the Ascended Masters bring through what's needed for each session. There can be dynamic downloads, activations, guidance, or clearing/healing. Here is the testimonial of one of the participants:

> *Thank you again for the meditation on Saturday. Whatever cleared out of the right side of my head has allowed my energy to even out. I can feel energy moving freely on that side of my body now. Many thanks for facilitating! The most wonderful thing is I'm not sure I ever had energetic access to this portion of my body. If I do, I don't remember the feeling. Everything on the right side of my face feels open and flowing. Even my hearing seems better! (Sara; California, USA)*

Apart from what's been previously mentioned, portal energy is also very powerful for manifestation. I have developed some unique manifestation techniques that, by going to the high-dimension realm and performing the visualisation and clearing blocks, have proven to be effective and profound.

The most recent example is in December 2022—one of the 369 portal days, which also happened to be my fiftieth Solar return—when I did a manifestation for finding a Soulmate during the meditation. Two days later, I actually came across my Soulmate in a Facebook group, but we didn't communicate until five weeks later when one of his posts kept showing up. This prompted me to make contact, and we instantly discovered a deep connection on the Soul level. Less than four weeks since we had first made contact, I flew over twelve thousand miles to the other side of the globe to meet him. This Soulmate meets most of the aspects of an ideal partner I have been hoping for. If the manifestation techniques can help me to achieve what I've been looking for, I believe this tool can help others too!

For more information about portal meditation and free events:

https://www.awakeningwithjoy.com/events

Connect with Me!

I am now inspired to work as an energy healer, reader, and intuitive coach ever more in true alignment with my Higher Self, no longer attached to false self-identification. I no longer conform to the expectations and false reflections of those figures in my life who, as well as showing me love—also without my conscious awareness—kept me in a state of limitation and false identification.

It is my honour on my spiritual path to be helping others to release their karmic baggage and what's surfacing to be cleared and healed. Showing the way for my clients, and sharing my journey in an act of service, is so fulfilling to me. It is much more fulfilling and important to my soul than any temporary distractions I had when focussed on the attachments of a conventional life and material goals! I have truly found my calling, and I am grateful each day for my work, for discovering my life's purpose, and for embodying my Higher Self.

I am grateful for my opportunity in this life to work on my soul realignment and Ascension. I am equally grateful to be helping others to transcend limitations and break free of karmic patterns that hold them back from the soul-affirming, conscious life we all deserve! I am always available to work in service for the highest good to assist in bringing clients to a place of spiritual change and true energetic clarity!

When I now work with clients, helping them to clear karmic ties which bind them to lower energetic matrices and limit their life choices, I am also honouring and celebrating my liberation. With each client I help, I also am liberated from the limitations of who I felt I was supposed to be as a child.

Every moment spent on my spiritual work, I transcend the limitation of being the boy I never could be for my mother, the child who could only experience fear when tuning into spiritual frequencies and was overwhelmed with others' energies. Through my work, I am honouring the path of surrendering lower desires in this life, to reconnect with who we all are, collectively, as beings of light. And I am honouring and celebrating that our true heritage and spiritual home is not the earth, but higher realms, higher planes of existence.

It's my passion to share my healing and spiritual growth journey in my blogs and Facebook posts. In addition, I offer free meditation and energy transmission on my YouTube channel to help people on the same path, who could benefit from hearing my insights on spirituality and to experience the energetic work I transmit. Many people have benefited from the meditation and manifestation videos on my YouTube channel. I offer group meditation on special portal days and facilitate the transmission of pure portal energies. You are most welcome to make a connection with me through the following social media platforms:

Joy Vottus, Australia

Website & Blog: https://www.awakeningwithjoy.com/

Facebook Group: https://www.facebook.com/groups/awakeningwithjoy/

YouTube: https://youtube.com/c/AwakeningwithJoy

Instagram: https://www.instagram.com/joy333.awakening.ascend/

Chapter Six

All Our Answers Lie Within: Healing Through Love and Forgiveness

by Jan Thompson

Self-empowerment is the big lesson here on Earth.

-St. Germain

Small Beginnings

I have been on my Ascension journey my whole life. Some of the time I was unconscious of my journey. At other times I was very conscious and purposeful of my journey. I became very committed to my Ascension over the past ten or more years when I discovered Verna and Waireti and the Alpha Imaging website in New Zealand.

When I was very young, I remember telling my mom I could see particles in the air around me. They looked like the tiniest of diamonds. I always thought they were so beautiful but had no idea what they were. My mom was very open, and never once did she say that I was imagining things or making them up, but she couldn't see what

I saw. I believe now that they were adamantine particles—particles of love and light. I understand adamantine particles to be God particles. Glenda Green channels Jesus in her book, *Love Without End: Jesus Speaks*. In the book, Jesus explains that the adamantine particles are infinity particles that create substance, or mass. Looking back, I find it hard to believe I could have seen something so infinitely tiny. I think young children can "see" things that we can't as adults.

I also remember a road trip I took with my parents as a young child, likely four or five years old. There were two different places we traveled to that none of us had been to before. I distinctly remember saying to my mom, "Oh, I remember this place—I have been here before." I remembered a particular building and Mount Rushmore. It was the first trip there for my entire family.

I remember being a fourteen-year-old girl studying in confirmation classes. I would debate with the minister and ask many questions, staying late after everyone else had left. I was not taking anything at face value and wanted to understand things in my own way. I felt that there was a greater truth to be learned. My confirmation day arrived, and it was my turn to approach the minister. During the confirmation I felt a rush through my body, a body shiver and awakening of sorts, to unlimited and expansive love that filled my heart. I felt the energy of a greater power moving through my body. I felt like I floated back to my seat.

I became an elementary school teacher and administrator before my children were born. I studied a variety of disciplines to use in my classroom. I taught children with learning disabilities, physical disabilities, refugees who could not speak English and who had come from traumatic situations, and children who were blind and used braille to read and write. Besides what I had been taught in university, there had to be other ways to communicate and reach these little beings. I remember learning Edu-K to help with learning challenges and help everyone to feel calmer and more confident. I learned a new way to teach children with dyslexia to read. To this day, I believe that dyslexia is a gift that allows the dyslexic to see from all sides of a situation and all points of view. Any time I tried something "outside the box," I would see the excitement in the children and the joy they felt about their accomplishments.

As I got older, my mom would come to me if she was feeling down or unwell and ask me to place my hands on her. She said that I had "healing hands." She would tell my siblings that I had healing hands, and they accepted that it was true. I thought my mom was being complimentary and didn't know what to believe. As I became more interested in healing modalities, I also began to believe in myself and my own gifts more and more. I took courses in Therapeutic Touch and Reiki, Reflexology, light, and colour therapy, and explored my interests in Homeopathy and Bach flower remedies. I would use the different healing modalities on our children when they became ill or had an injury. My family became used to me pulling out all the stops when it came to helping them feel better and get well.

When Mom was diagnosed with cancer and had a breast removed, I was the one she called upon to give her Therapeutic Touch or just lay my hands on her to help with her healing and recovery. We worked together to create positive affirmations and a positive mindset. My mom credited this extra "healing work" as being instrumental in her healing.

At one time, my mom's friend was in the hospital with terminal cancer. The family asked if I would come in to provide some relief for their mother during her last days. The attending physician approved my visit. He was astounded after the healing session the following day. My mom's friend was in a much more comfortable and peaceful state than she had been before the healing sessions. The family was so grateful for the relief that had been provided for their mother. Healing does not always mean that the person will be rid of cancer or the disease or physical limitation, but it can mean that emotional or inner healing has taken place and the person is at peace with themselves.

We Can Heal Ourselves

All the while, I kept feeling that it was not just me who was providing the healing and relief, but something working through me; something powerful, yet calming at the same time. Whatever it was, I was grateful I could be of service in some way. I also realized how miraculous our bodies are. Our body knows how to heal itself if given the chance and the love, energy, and positivity it deserves. Its mission is to return to its original divine blueprint. Sometimes a person does not heal from a particular physical illness or injury but can come to a place of love, peace, and harmony within themselves. Our physical body is the vessel we inhabit for our life here on Earth. Other aspects of ourselves can be healed for our continued journey as a soul.

I believe that we come to this beautiful earthly plane with a predetermined plan for our life. Sometimes it is to experience a short life or a life with pain or disease; a life with its own challenges. Regardless, we can heal emotionally, spiritually, and throughout our ancestry while we are here.

Healing in these areas is about clearing karma. This is what Ascension is all about. Clearing karma and not creating more karma for ourselves. I have come to learn this over the past ten to fifteen years of my life. We come to live on this earth as wounded and "wounding" human beings over many lifetimes. We choose the families we are born into. We choose who we incarnate with to provide lessons to learn from, clear from our energy fields, and not repeat. The more we clear and release from our past lives and through our ancestry, the clearer and more radiant our chakras become. Soon, when they are clear and purely radiant, we pass through a certain initiation level that does not require us to return to Earth. We do not need to reincarnate any longer. When this happens, our Higher Self wholly resides within us and becomes our partner in service for the rest of our physical life on earth. Notice I have said, "Our partner in service." Once the Higher Self fully embodies us, it is us, the lower self, who surrenders to the service of the Higher Self. We align with the service of our Higher Self. After years of conscious ascension and clearing my energy fields, I have the amazing opportunity to be fully partnered with my Higher Self in service. As a seventh Initiate, my Higher Self is now fully embodied and resides in my heart. I feel the great love that resides within me and can feel my Higher Self's great love for me. All my thoughts about healing and being human have proven to be true throughout my life. My Higher Self has shown me this over and over. We are all connected through our energetic resonance, through love, with Source, with God.

My Higher Self

My Higher Self, Pukalani, is on the green aspect of the fifth ray of knowledge, truth, and healing. When I realized he was on the fifth ray, I was not surprised. I felt it made sense after the years I had spent as a seeker, educator, and healer that all of my learning and exploration was to prepare me for this path of service with my Higher Self. My Higher Self is here to help humanity with self-empowerment. Human beings have been giving away their power and seeking truth outside themselves for millennia.

Pukalani is quiet, serious, and subtle in his communication, but it is through his gentle strength that he assists those who are struggling to come into their own power and truth, especially those who find it difficult to speak their truth. He can help you to find your truth within, thus helping you to find your strength and means to self-heal. He says, "Knowing yourself is knowing your truth." On a deeper level, he sees the inner conflict that exists within some of you, and he will help you resolve this. This will lead you not only to a place of greater self-understanding and healing, but also to a place of personal wisdom. If you could visualize him, he would appear as a powerful-looking Polynesian man with long dark hair and a beautiful, strong gaze. He wears an emerald-green tunic. On the sides and back of his head he wears a half circlet, from which silver and green crystals rise like two mountains on the side of his head, symbolizing the difficult climb of Ascension. He tells us to find the truth within, that all our answers lie within us, that we all can heal ourselves, and that we have the answers to our questions. Everything I do with my Higher Self is about self-empowerment in some way or another.

Healing Work

I trained in Usui Reiki years ago and now have added the Holy Fire® III, Karuna Reiki® to my learnings. The combination of Holy Fire® and Karuna Reiki® adds the energies of Ascended Masters Jesus and Kuan Yin to facilitate the healing session with my Higher Self. I love the idea of bringing the energies of other Ascended Masters to my practice. These energy healings are based on the idea of self-empowerment. During an energy healing session, my Higher Self will determine if he works alone or calls upon other Ascended Masters to facilitate the process. I hold the space and act as the conduit for whoever shows up to help in the healing process. I always ask that my Higher Self, Pukalani, relay to me what the recipient needs and receives so that I can communicate this after the session. Sometimes what a person thinks they need may surprise them because it is not always what they get, or they get much more than expected.

I think the bottom line with any of the work I do is that my true essence is working with my Higher Self. My ego and personality are not present. I begin all sessions by asking my personality and ego to step aside and wait for me while we do our work. By doing this, I can eliminate the static noise that can interrupt a pure connection. I then take the time to settle down into my Sacred Heart and Holy Heart. The Sacred Heart and Holy Heart are places within each of us where we can experience pure love and compassion, where we connect with Higher Self and serve in loving presence. I access my Sacred Heart and Holy Heart through breathwork and intention. I know when I have arrived because I am no longer interrupted by little pokings of thought, little interruptions that flit across my mind. My body tells me when I have arrived. Without the noisy static and mental chatter, Pukalani and I can tune in to the person, animal, place, or thing and focus on what is needed. It is then that I know what is required. Messages will pop up. I know whether I need to use tuning forks, toning, crystal bowls, crystals, etc., I just allow the energy to flow where it needs to go and how much time to take. I have been told that my true essence is one of deep peace. My Higher Self brings this energetic aspect to every healing session. He is the frequency of love and peace.

We are all energy. We are energetic beings of varying vibratory frequencies and are connected to everyone and everything in our energetic field. There is no separation between us. There is only the illusion of separateness. In a healing session, the loving energy flows and allows healing for whatever is in the recipient's highest good.

Chakra Clearing

Our chakras are where we store our karma. Our chakras can become misaligned and filled with dross; cluttered negative energy. My Higher Self can determine if the chakras need realigning or clearing some of the dross. I remember working with Terry over the course of several sessions. These sessions involved clearing out and realigning his chakras. During the third session, I quickly realized that the chakras were pristine, and some had actually disappeared! I knew then that Terry had gone through an initiation level where all the karma had been paid and cleared!

The chakras can also be associated with the energy systems of our physical body. Each chakra can relate to a nerve complex from our spinal column that enervates particular body systems and organs. For instance, the sacral chakra is associated with the bladder, reproductive organs, and kidneys, to name a few. The chakras can reflect what is going on in the nervous system, and thus our physical bodies.

I had a recent healing session with Mary, a menopausal woman. I perceived that her sacral chakra had a lot of dross and was out of alignment. My Higher Self was able to clear the dross and realign the chakra. I also detected that Mary's hormonal system was out of whack—it needed to be harmonized and balanced. My Higher Self guided me to attune the sacral and third eye chakras to each other. The master gland, the pituitary, is related to the third eye chakra. The other thing that came to my awareness was an emotional blockage around feeling unsupported. This blockage had physically manifested in the kidneys. The kidneys are related to the sacral chakra through the water element. There is so much interconnectedness within our bodies. It is truly miraculous!

Past Life and Ancestral Healing

As I mentioned before, we all have had many past lives on this Earth. Some of our past lives were not as pleasant or fulfilling as others. In some lives, we were victims or wounded emotionally and/or physically. In other lives, we were the perpetrators or the wounders. Any trauma experienced during these past lives can leave emotional blockages that can be passed on through cellular memory within our bodies. Sometimes these emotional wounds can be passed on through our ancestral lineage. Emotional blockages will reveal themselves to be cleared and healed.

Sonya held in her cellular memory the emotional wounding her grandmother had experienced. The wounding was passed on from the grandmother, through the mother, to the daughter. By clearing these blockages from Sonya's energy bodies, the healing cleared her past generations and generations to come. What a gift to give our children and their children! Not carrying the wounding from our past lives or our ancestors.

Current Life Trauma

My Higher Self has also helped clients to heal from trauma originating in this lifetime. Sometimes healing from a past life or ancestral life is easier to deal with. We don't need to know the story, and we feel somewhat detached from it—we don't feel that it was actually the current us, in the present, that experienced a particular situation in the past. It can be a different matter when we are living it in the here and now.

My Higher Self and I were able to help Valerie, who had experienced two stillbirths, one after the other. These were extremely traumatic events for her on many levels; physically, mentally, and emotionally. Through many sessions of reiki and energy work, she was able to work through her grief as well as her physical pain. Of course, Valerie experienced the pain on all levels. It took time to allow for the grief to pave the way for healing to take place. My Higher Self and various Ascended Masters brought love, compassion, gentle patience, and empathy to her sessions. Mental and emotional healing enabled physical healing to take place.

A unique situation presented itself when Ruth came to me after her son had taken his own life. She was still very connected to her son, both emotionally and physically. Even though he had passed, she still felt the attachment and connection to him in a particular area of her body. After a couple of healing sessions, we were able to release his attachment to her from her physical body. Ruth fell into a deep sleep during the session. After the healing session, Ruth told me that she felt her son had been attached to the left side of her torso, and when she awoke, the attachment was gone. Now he can communicate with her emotionally and spiritually, in a purely loving way. This was a much more harmonious outcome for her. Ruth can continue living her life knowing that her son will always be with her, but not physically dependent upon her energy. Our loved ones who have passed can continue communicating with and guiding us in healthier, more loving ways.

Entities and Spirit Attachments

Unwanted entities and spirit attachments are very common. As humans clear their karma, become more radiant, and vibrate at a higher frequency, we become attractive beacons for negativity. Think of how moths are attracted to light. When we turn off the light, the moths and insects disperse. Turn on the light, and they are drawn to it like a magnet. So it goes with entities and spirits. Spirit attachments are often souls who have passed but are reluctant to return to Source. It could be that they became confused upon death if it was sudden, such as in an accident. They can also feel very drawn to a person or the place they lived and want to hang around because it is familiar. This can be very disconcerting for those alive on the physical plane. Most people have attachments—or hitchhikers, as I like to call them. They can sap our energy, confuse us, and affect our mental and emotional bodies. Once these bodies are affected, issues can then manifest in the physical body. We become ill, develop disease, and feel unwell or not like our usual selves.

Entities are often picked up in the Astral realm, either when we sleep, daydream, or occasionally because we choose to go there. Some people feel that if they can travel to the Astral realm, they are having a spiritual experience. This is far from the truth. Most beings in the Astral realm are of low vibrational frequency and will latch on to any unsuspecting visitor. These entities are mischievous, and some can be downright malevolent. It is wise to identify them and release and clear them once and for all.

My Higher Self can determine if a client has an entity. Often I will work via the phone, or on a call with the client to help remove an entity. It can be very empowering to identify the entity and have help cutting the cords and releasing the negative energy to Love and Light. I will relay the experience I had with one client.

Brandi knew she had an entity and contacted me for its release and clearing. My Higher Self and I connected with Brandi and talked her through the process. She could identify and describe the entity—give it a size, colour, and shape. Doing this helps to create a visual for release. I asked Brandi to use her intention to put the entity into a box and hand it over to the two Ascended Masters I had connected with to assist in the healing session. They returned the entity to the Love and Light while my Higher Self held a higher vibrational space for the release to take place. It took a while. Some entities can be very persistent—but often half the work is being willing to accept that one is attached and then release it. In this case, the entity was gone within an hour. Once the entity is cleared, there can be a feeling of grief or sadness on the part of the client. An important part of the removal process is to heal the area where the attachment had been. I often call upon St. Germain to purify and transmute any leftover energy to love and light. I also call upon Mother Mary to fill the area with unconditional love. Love and light will help the wound from the attachment to heal.

Every healing session brings about healing, whether small with baby steps or grand with a major shift. The healing energy comes through in the frequency of love. One of the key components of healing is love and forgiveness for self and others. We have all been and done many things in our lives here on Earth. Seemingly insignificant events can have a major impact on another person and ourselves. We cannot measure one wrongdoing to have more impact than another. It is not about judgment. It is about the love and forgiveness we can extend to ourselves and others. The greatest gift we can give ourselves is to love ourselves unconditionally. Only then can we truly love others. Love paves the way for self-empowerment as we come to know ourselves and our divine destiny. In love, we can move forward on our life's journey.

For further information on Reiki and energy healing sessions, please visit www.ascensionarts.ca.

Ascension Dowsing

I have been a dowser for about ten years. My friend Carol Anne Halstead and I co-founded Ascension Dowsing. We created our unique Dowsing method after realizing that the method we had been taught could be cumbersome and awkward. We no longer had to be onsite to detect hidden things that can cause disturbances. No longer did we have to be on-site to correct these disturbances. We no longer had to leave tools and devices in place to maintain the corrections. We developed our unique method. When the global pandemic prevented us from entering other people's homes, we could continue our practice remotely, without interruption.

We dowse remotely and create beautifully sanctified and energized properties through the use of intention and sacred geometry. The amazing sacred geometric shape of the octahedron encircled within a sphere is what we energetically anchor around the property according to the four directions. We then program the octahedron. Once it is anchored and programmed by us, we invite the client to complete the programming with their intentions for their living space. In his film, *The Missing Gods,* Freddy Silva has said that the octahedron is the most accurate shape for us as humans to see all perspectives. The octahedron is the sacred shape that holds the attributes of harmony and balance. Harmony and balance are created within a home or property we have dowsed. Through Ascension Dowsing, we have cleared and elevated the energy levels in more than sixty-five homes worldwide. We must live in a safe and nurturing environment to feel empowered, safe, and nurtured. Ascension Dowsing creates this environment within your home, property, workplace, or small area; anywhere you spend a lot of time and need to feel at peace, relaxed, and supported. You can be living and working in a self-empowering environment!

Carol Anne has relayed several stories in her chapter about how dowsing has changed the day-to-day lives of our clients. I will add some stories here that show how Dowsing has provided self-empowerment to those who asked for our services.

Clearing Karma

Often people can be drawn to a certain place to resolve issue(s) in their life, though they may not always be aware of this. Dowsing can bring up karmic lines for those living within the home. One of the last things we determine is if any karma shows up for any of the residents. Sometimes there is a karmic line for an individual. Sometimes there is a karmic line that involves the whole family. Remember when I said that we often reincarnate with the same people over lifetimes? That is where a family or group karmic line can come up for clearing. In one particular situation, Carol Anne and I were asked to dowse the condo and condo building for Clara. After dowsing the building, we then dowsed the individual condo. We found that there was a karmic line that had revealed itself for clearing. As seventh initiates, we can clear karma for others through our Higher Selves. In this instance, we asked if we were to clear the karma, and we got a "no." We did not ask about the karmic line—it was not our business.

Clara's husband was not present at this time. Clara suspected that the karmic line had something to do with her husband's relationship with her mother, his mother-in-law. So we left it.

Two years later, Clara asked us to come back to address another issue. We checked to see if the karmic line was still present for her husband. It was not. Clara told us that her husband had repaired the relationship with his mother-in-law! Simply by discovering the husband's karmic line, energy had been created to clear the karmic debt. He was energetically empowered to do so!

Discovering a Stargate!

Lisa had recently purchased a property that she was drawn to all her life, and now her dream of owning the property was fulfilled. There was a reason she was meant to purchase this property. The property consisted of two large buildings and extensive grounds behind the buildings. We found an anomaly on the grounds behind the buildings; something we had never discovered before. There were a series of positive vortexes in a circle formation. The energy of this section of the land was extremely high—higher than anything we had ever measured before.

We dowsed extensively and found out that the energetic circle, a Stargate, had been created by Pleiadeans prior to Atlantean and Lemurian times! Crystals had been placed deep underground, anchoring the divine feminine energy to the Earth at this place. Renovations were currently underway in the large building that was Lisa's home. She intended to create a sacred retreat space for goddess ceremonies in a newly constructed building on the grounds. We received the message that the land where the Stargate was located would provide the energy for her sacred ceremony centre, but that it was not to be disturbed. Luckily, we were able to find this out before any construction had begun. The land was left as is.

Today, the high vibrational centre for goddess ceremonies and healings has been created within one of the original buildings. Quite recently, we discovered that the Sirians are also using this Stargate. Lisa and another high Initiate who are in service on the property have a direct connection to one of the guardians of the Stargate! These discoveries would likely not have been revealed if construction had taken place!

Angelic Portal!

Another anomaly! It is not very often that we find sacred portals on a property. We found one on the large property owned by Lori Diebold, who works with angels in her healing practice. Lori also shares her stories in another chapter of this book. The sacred portal had such a high reading that we could not measure it. A positive portal is an opening, or doorway, to another dimension. This portal was a doorway to the angelic realm! How perfect to discover this. We guided Lori on how this portal might be used to communicate with the angels and further her higher service even more.

Happy Employees, Happy Customers

When your place of employment is supportive and high-vibrational, your work is more productive and of high quality. Tom, a small business owner, contacted us to dowse his business. Tom specifically noted that he had troubles with his employees. The employees were not getting along. Jobs were not being done well. As a result, customer service and satisfaction suffered, and there was a high employee absence rate.

The beauty of the sacred geometry anchored around the property during the dowsing process is that it provides the right level of vibrational frequency for everyone living or working in the space. It is a great leveler! Remember, those are the qualities of the octahedron—to balance and harmonize. Once the property was dowsed, the employees became more relaxed and cooperative. Tom had to intervene less and less to make peace among the employees. One or two of the employees left of their own accord. Tom was able to hire people who thrived in the higher energetic vibe of the company. A new company culture was created that was evident in the employees' satisfaction with their work. Tom reported that the employees felt a sense of pride in their work, and Tom felt a sense of peace and cooperation among the employees. Customer service improved. Happy customers, happy employees!

Finding True Love

Sometimes all it takes is the pure intention from the heart, in the creation point, to manifest what you truly desire. Gail had called in 2021 for us to dowse her home and property and bring it up to a nurturing and supportive level for her. She wanted to create a space where Love could grow as she anticipated someone to share her life with. We dowsed her home, clearing away any disturbances through the use of sacred geometry. Gail was very invested in setting her intentions for the property and her life going forward. She also booked a Personal Octahedron session while we completed her home dowsing. We were not told what Gail's personal programming was for her home and PO, but within two weeks she met the person who is currently her life partner. To this day, Gail credits the programming and intention-setting of her octahedron for this beautiful and welcome change to her life.

All our dowsing work is done from a place of love and inner knowing. Carol Anne and I work together on each project after we have connected Sacred Heart to Sacred Heart. We then connect to the space we are dowsing. Coming to each project from love with our Higher Selves allows for accurate answers and information to come through. We are so amazed and grateful that we can help others this way.

For further information on Ascension Dowsing, please visit:

www.ascensiondowsing.com

Personal Octahedron

The Personal Octahedron, or PO, is something that came about during my healing sessions. I would instinctively set up an energetic octahedron around my client at the end of a healing session. It would hold the energy as it continued to heal over time. I always wondered why the energetic shape didn't remain around the client. In a channeled session with Courtney Dillon, I asked St. Germain why the PO was not permanent. He said it was because the person is not activating it themselves. You may have noticed the quote by St. Germain at the beginning of my chapter, "Self-Empowerment is the big lesson here on Earth." Well, I learned that the energetic container I envisioned around my Reiki clients needed to be programmed by them for it to become permanent.

The PO is an energetic container that, once programmed, has many functions. It is a frequency filter that only allows positive high vibrational energy to enter it. It becomes a protection grid against negative entities and spirits. It becomes a grounding device keeping us firmly rooted to Mother Earth. It becomes a harmonizing container balancing divine feminine and divine masculine energies creating divine unity within. It holds only our gifts and blessings from the past without the negative trauma. It helps keep us in line with our perfect path, our divine destiny. The energy within the octahedron is transmuted by St. Germain and filled with unconditional love by Mother Mary. The most important shape is the sphere; the geometric structure where cells are being created. To awaken the cell's power for healing, we need to go within. The octahedron is the container we can use to go within the sphere or cell. From there, we can truly change our cellular memory, heal, and become the best version of ourselves. As without, so within. We have an energetic octahedron around our physical body, and we can intend a personal octahedron of any size to go within and heal ourselves. It is truly amazing! And we can all have our own Personal Octahedron; our self-empowering device!

To learn more about the Personal Octahedron please visit www.ascensionarts.ca.

Self- Empowerment is Reclaiming Our Essence

Self-empowerment is our right, our gift. It is our knowledge of ourselves, the Truth of who we are and our purpose. It is to love and know our service here on Earth and claim it. We must recognize this strength within ourselves, knowing we can all be healers. We are miraculous beings capable of more than we know. Clearing karma, past life, and ancestral healing, healing our different energy bodies, healing current life situations and not creating more karma, and creating nurturing environments to live and thrive in is the way to see ourselves with clarity. Our love shines, and our true essence is revealed. Our Ascension journey can become a conscious one. We can recognize ourselves as the divine being we are and say, "This is who I am!"

Jan Thompson, Canada

Website: www.ascensiondowsing.com

Website: www.ascensionarts.ca

Facebook: https://www.facebook.com/ascensiondowsing

Chapter Seven

You've Got This

by Kimberley Roles

Just one small positive thought
in the morning
can change your whole day.

-Dalai Lama

Next time you think or feel that you're not making the kind of progress you'd hoped for toward a particular goal, take a moment to tell yourself: "You've got this." It's amazing the power these three little words can have, and it's wonderful to see how you can grow and learn through almost any situation masterfully. Such self-talk is a great way to activate the version of you who has amazing grit and an indomitable spirit.

If you are reading this book, it means you are on an awakening path, an Ascension journey, the process of moving from one level of your consciousness to another. It is a natural process that happens as part of a person's evolutionary experience through time and space.

In this chapter, I will tell you about the major events in my life that have influenced me toward positive change.

My Story

I believe so much transformation happens via inspiration; stories are often the vehicle we use to get there. Storytelling is an extremely powerful tool that can touch a heart, excite and motivate a mind, or if we're not careful, keep us from growing, changing, or creating. It's a powerful way to communicate and transfer feelings from one person to another. Most people lack time, the right mindset, clarity, and action when manifesting their dreams and purpose. As a heart-centered lightworker who has been there myself, I am here to help people transform lives from the ground up. People often need a transformational shift, and my goal is to help them overcome things I have struggled with in my personal life. I want to help people shine their light, feel good, have breakthroughs, and understand that they are the creators of their reality. I want to help them learn what being a Spirit living in a human body means. I don't want anyone to waste years like I did in life getting to that point.

The path of spiritual awakening is a journey. It's a crazy experience. It's an ever-evolving exploration of the true nature of our soul. The awakening process can be messy. It can be confusing. It is usually triggered by an event. Your world is shaken up. You might not know what's going on with you, but you sense a change and you're confused.

My awakening process began when I was sixteen. It is clear to me how much love and support are required to walk a true spiritual path. I know how challenging it can be to face the things we all wish we could just transcend—insecurity, fear, pride, envy, control, and self-judgment—as well as our stories of separation and hurt. There was a time when I felt so ashamed that I could still stumble back into old patterns despite having accessed refined spiritual states. But over the years I have learned how to meet my humanity with love, patience, and devotion to discovering what is and isn't true.

Becoming an Adult at Sixteen

Little did I know how much my life would change after my mom passed away when I was thirty-seven. I had been living life in a daily routine like everyone else I knew then. I had my son when I was sixteen years old; still in high school and living with my parents. We had been brought up in the Episcopal Church, and my mom was very involved with the Church: serving on the vestry, singing in the choir, and much more. I was petrified for her to find out I was pregnant and did not want either parent to know. However, that would not be a choice I would have to make. As "fate" would have it...I did not find out I was pregnant until I was five-and-a-half months along. Much to my surprise, my mom took it well. Of course, she cried for me, but she did not kick me out or make me give up my baby. She treated me as she always had, with love and respect. I didn't know she told my dad at first because he never acted any differently toward me. He continued to drive me to school, would give me a kiss on the forehead, and we, as a family, got on with life. I have a younger brother and two younger twin sisters.

Michael was born on January thirteenth, 1988, on a cold, snowy morning. He was late and I was going to be induced, but he came before that happened. I was not prepared for the pain I was experiencing in the middle of the night. I finally went into my parents' bedroom and told them I had pains that would not go away.

My mom asked how often they came, and I said, "About every five minutes."

She screamed, "Charley, get up! We must take Kim to the hospital."

I was seven-and-a-half centimeters dilated when I arrived, and no room was available. I thought I would have to deliver in the hallway. Luckily a room became available, and Michael was born at eleven thirty-four in the morning, weighing eight pounds, two ounces, and measuring twenty-one and three-quarters inches long.

That was the beginning of the rest of my life; where events would occur that would move me forward into my next season of expansion, focusing on my personal evolution (Ascension/ awakening journey) both physically and at a soul level.

So I continued living my three-D life. I finished high school and got a full-time job with medical benefits for my son and me. I went to college at night. I would come home, feed my son his bottle, get my homework done, and start all over the next day. When Michael started elementary school, I moved out of my parents' home and rented a duplex. Space was getting tight at my parents' house, and my sisters and brother were getting older and not wanting to stay home and babysit! I was blessed to have the help at home for as long as I did.

Yoga: A Huge Turning Point For Me

While living on my own, I started to experience stress, anxiety, and depression for various reasons. I was trying to live a normal life, have friends, go to work and school, and raise Michael. Getting him off to school became a struggle when he reached a certain age, as he became bored and did not want to go. I started seeing a psychologist, and Michael came with me many times. Eventually I realized that rehashing my issues was not helping anymore. My progressive psychologist suggested I consider taking yoga and/or meditation classes. He had a few different flyers of yoga studios in my area, and I picked one intuitively and signed up for a four-week introductory yoga class.

Upon completion, I immediately purchased a membership with the studio. I continued going there and took every class offered. I can't explain how great I felt and what a difference it made in my life. I attended meditation classes, received Reiki healings, and everything in between. I had an entirely new group of friends. I had a community and felt like a completely different person.

I then enrolled in teacher training and became a certified yoga instructor, Reiki master, meditation, and yoga nidra practitioner. My focus at the time of my yoga certification was teaching children. At the time I had young nieces and nephews who were very interested in watching me while I practiced yoga. I found a children's yoga instructor nearby in my town. I enrolled in her class and started my own kids' yoga classes afterward. Kids across the globe are living through a historic time that is devastatingly impacting their mental health and well-being. And unfortunately, there are not enough services and resources to reach out and help. Now more than ever, kids need strong, caring, and supportive adults to help guide them, ground them, and show them that there is still magic in the world. To teach them that it is okay to play and have fun! Unfortunately, I had to end my live classes in 2020 due to Covid. I am reviving these classes now, and by the time this book is in print, I hope to have a kids' yoga class workshop available online for all ages and levels!

These practices helped me get through the unexpected passing of my mom. She had just turned sixty. I was thirty-seven. She had been diagnosed with adult-onset diabetes and eventually developed neuropathy in her legs and was wheelchair-bound. Although we knew she was sick and were taking care of her, we did not expect her to pass so quickly and were unprepared. She passed in the night sometime before Church one Sunday morning. My dad came down to get her dressed and make her breakfast, but she was gone. I no longer had a mother in the physical. I was a mess and didn't know what to do with myself.

My First Psychic Reading

A couple of months after my mom's passing, I became obsessed with finding a psychic medium to get in touch with her on the "other side." I had never been to one before, as we were taught in Church that anything psychic was "the work of the devil." I went online and searched for the best of the best. I didn't know how a psychic could reach my mom if they were not in person with me. I was still naïve about energy, our souls, the truth of who we are and where we come from. I settled on a psychic from Texas and had my first reading ever over the phone (this was before Zoom, Skype, etc.). I still have the CD recording she gave me from that reading in 2009. She gave me proof that my mom came through with information that there was no way she could have known...starting with her name and the fact that I had her nails painted for her while she lay in her coffin. And there were so many other messages that she brought through to my family and me. This was a great comfort to us all. This woman would become a friend, a spiritual teacher, and a mentor. She set me off on another path of spiritual evolution, expansion, and Ascension.

We Create Our Own Reality

After a few readings with Jennifer, I set up calls for my dad (a non-believer). But he felt so much relief after hearing these messages that only my mother could have given that we actually attended a few in-person events when Jennifer would be anywhere in the New England area. I also purchased her CDs for meditation and began using them regularly. She introduced me to Abraham Hicks, the author of *Getting into the Vortex*. This book reminded me that we create our own reality. He says we have a vortex of everything we have ever called into our life, and it is just waiting for us to align with it and claim it. This blew my mind and life wide open to possibilities I had never thought possible. I tried to explain this to my family and friends, but they were not ready at the time to hear this and could not even comprehend what I was talking about. So I continued reading, listening, journaling, and soaking up all I could.

Next, she introduced me to Dr. Wayne Dyer. Dyer has another term for the concept behind the Law of Attraction. He calls it the Power of Intention. His philosophy is pure and simple, "The law of attraction is this: You don't attract what you want. You attract what you are." I have taught and continue to teach many classes on manifesting, the Law of Attraction, and creating your own reality. I wish the whole world could understand this concept. I have manifested many things in my life, which still amazes me because they are always things I want or need, but don't cling to. I don't "pray really hard" —I "hang on loosely," and those seem to be the things that appear in my life quickly. For instance, I recently went on a spiritual retreat to Sedona. A retreat opportunity came up, and since I was now newly single, I wanted to get away, clear my mind, and be in the healing energy of Sedona. I mentioned it to my boss to make sure I could get the time off, and not only did I get the time off, but he used his credit card rewards to pay for my airfare, hotel, and car rental to the airport!

I had an amazing experience, and while I was there, the retreat leader (whom the Universe also brought to me in very serendipitous ways once I started my awakening), announced during the trip that she would be leading her final journey to Egypt in the coming months. I paid no attention, because it was not on my bucket list of places to go, and I did not think it would be something I would do by myself. However, the Universe tends to send you where you are supposed to be and can move people, places, and things to make things happen. So one day I received a call while I was in the shower from a girl that was on my trip to Sedona. She left me a message asking if I intended to go to Egypt because she was considering it. It was pricier than going to Sedona and was a two-week trip. It also meant that I would have to fly by myself internationally. But I sent the retreat leader a message and inquired whether the spaces were filled for the trip to Egypt, and she replied, "Wow! Sedona must have really shifted you, LOL!" I got the information from her, and I had almost three months to prepare, pack, and pay for this journey that most of the other journeyers had been preparing a year for. She told me how much she needed for the down payment to hold my space, and I told her I would let her know by the end of the week if it was a go.

Now let me go back to my son for a minute...my son has grown up and chosen the path of an activist of sorts. His work is saving the environment, the planet, and many people. Many years ago, Michael was telling me he was working on fighting the payday loan companies that took advantage of people who needed money. These people were paying high interest on their loans that they could never catch up with because the loan companies were attaching their pay for payment. I explained to him that I would never have wanted him to know this when he was younger, but I was, in fact, one of those people. There was a time when I was working and not making enough money to pay our rent, utilities, and to put food on the table as a single mother. I took out a payday loan, and they sucked up my entire paycheck to pay it back, forcing me to take out another loan to have money, and it went on and on. He asked if I would write a letter about my story so he could present it as part of his case. I did. That was many years ago. The week that I made the decision that I may want to go to Egypt, I received what I thought was one of those fake checks you get in the mail (but you really have to call an eight hundred number, which turns into a loan), so I almost threw it away. But I opened it, and it was a check for my share of a settlement from the payday loan companies case Michael had represented many years ago. I called him right away to see if it was real, and it was. The check was for the exact amount that I needed for my down payment to secure my spot for the Egypt retreat! I took that as a sign that I was supposed to go to Egypt. I did, and it all worked out, and I had many incredible expanding moments. The other interesting thing is

I had no idea how the company that sent the check had the correct address, as I had moved three times since I wrote that letter.

I could go on and on with manifestations such as that...they are available to all of us. I get messages from clients who have attended one of my classes or purchased a masterclass online with some of their results. Here is a message I received from one of my clients. Megan wrote, "So I have to share this craziness with you! I have been stressing a little about finances with moving the office and the apartment, and there was an issue with my tax return with the money we planned on using. We both (her and her partner) tried to remind each other that it would work out. It always does! Long story short, we got a text at eight pm tonight that her tax return was credited to her credit card. Craziness! I feel like I was driving home enlightened and positive that great things are coming. Holy %$#! This works fast!"

Tracy wrote: "OMG...So I just did your money meditation, and towards the end, suddenly I could SEE the energy you've been talking about. It was blue/purplish and orange/reddish/yellowish... all moving around like a heated lava lamp...it was crazy and awesome all at the same time." Tracy originally started coming to my meditation workshops and then came to me because she wanted to start her own business and quit her current job. She was out of work with a medical injury and took this time to work on herself and her beliefs around money, and to do some coaching with me. She went on to open her own business as a single mother. Now her kids are working with her, and she is making more money in her own business, making her own hours, and spending more time with her children than she did when she was working as a nurse. And she is no longer suffering injuries due to the intense labor of the job.

Synchronicity in Florida

Law Of Attraction: Like Attracts Like

When you're on the right path and passionate about your work, the universe conspires with you because you're aligned with Source energy. You become part of the creative process.

It is often said that we are "spiritual beings living a human experience." I was still living on this three-D Earth, experiencing all the emotions. Both fun and happy times and a fair share of sad and upsetting times. I experienced heartbreak and breakups. At this time, one had me in a state of unworthiness and depression. I know we create our own reality, and I want to keep my vibration in alignment with what it is I want to receive. Once you open yourself up to this new level of consciousness, all kinds of people walk into your life at the right times. An intuitive friend told me I needed to take a trip somewhere out of state alone to be in my own energy, away from others, and have time to think and explore. I had no idea where to go, and the thought of traveling alone frightened me. I don't know what made me choose this area in Florida, but I found a house on VRBO. It was on Florida's gulf coast, an area I had never been to. I booked the flights and everything else, took a taxi from the airport, stayed in this little house on the beach (which I love), and settled in.

I had no car while there, and I walked the street and the path on the beach. Everything I pretty much needed, which wasn't much, was within walking distance. One day, as I was walking down the street past a bookstore, I saw a flier in the window advertising that a woman would be in the store doing small group readings and meditations. I was thrilled when I saw her name and picture on the flier...YES! It was the medium from Texas, Jennifer. I went to the bookstore to meet her, and it turns out she was now living there. She moved from Texas to Florida because she received a message from her guides that this was where she was supposed to be. So I was able to spend time with her, and she introduced me to other like-minded people that became friends that I would spend time with, as I continued to visit there once a year. That trip was exactly what I needed to clear my mind and emotional body and bring me the clarity I needed then.

Intuition, Tarot, and the Story of Brooke's Baby

As we move into new levels of consciousness (and continue to alchemize any hidden parts of the shadow), we begin to experience new levels of physical and mental awareness, skills, and abilities in ways we never dreamed possible.

After that initial reading with my psychic, Jennifer, I researched independently and took classes to develop and open my intuition. Through my study, I learned that if we simply "allow," we can all turn on our psychic or intuitive abilities.

You can tap into your intuition in numerous ways, and like any other skill, practice is key. It's vital to have the discipline to practice every day. It's also important to set aside a time daily when you can be alone, undisturbed. I practiced using Tarot cards for myself and my friends before going public or charging for a Tarot reading. In 2020, I offered a "Year Preview for 2021" reading, and while I was doing a reading for a client, I was almost afraid to tell her what I had drawn for her. I knew her but knew nothing about her personal life. One of the cards indicated that she or someone close to her would be expecting a child in 2021. I knew her age and that she had one child already, but I was not expecting what she had to tell me next. She told me that no one at all knew except for her and her husband that they had been trying to conceive a child. They were not having luck and didn't think it would happen. She was overjoyed by that message. To take it one step further...she did get pregnant soon after this reading. I had a dream one night from her "spirit baby," who asked me to ask her mom to write her a letter, telling her what her life would be like when she got here! I was a little nervous to give her that message, but Brooke did give birth to a perfectly healthy baby girl on October eighteenth, 2021.

I am still offering these readings throughout the year; it does not have to be at the start of the New Year. I also offer an online, "Go at your own pace" Tarot reading workshop on my website if you are interested in learning yourself.

Meditation

Meditation is a tool we can use to better access our higher self—our soul self, also known as our pure conscious state. When we take time to meditate, we return to our center and can truly rest and remember that we are not our work, ego, or even our minds. We're simply beautiful, infinite observers of reality.

As I said previously, my psychologist recommended meditation years ago. I didn't believe it would be possible to stop my monkey mind. But it changed my life, and I teach and assist clients using meditations all the time. My meditations have specific sound frequencies and meanings that soothe the senses and facilitate greater mindfulness. Meditations are designed to give the mind an object to focus on. When you have an object of focus, it becomes easier to steady the mind.

Meditation can be a transformative practice. It is an excellent way to:

- Open and balance your chakras.
- Concentrate your energy.
- Boost self-knowledge.
- Develop your psychic awareness.
- Help pave the way for emotional healing.

For example, here is what my client had to say after an hour-long yoga nidra meditation. This person suffers from insomnia and wanted to give it a try. "I have been wanting to text you for a few days...the last meditation, the energy was so crazy in that room, it was so strong that I never really went under; I did, however, sleep amazingly well that night...almost like a continuation of your meditation, and I woke up feeling like we had just finished up! Crazy! Thanks again."

In this meditation, there was also an activation to help release from your awareness anything that is no longer serving you while practicing yoga nidra. Since this testimonial, I have worked with this client who, at the time, was having trouble concentrating in school and having relationship issues with her mother. She has now graduated from college and is working in the field where she is pursuing further studies. She no longer feeds into the issues with her mother. She has set boundaries and can have an actual "relationship" with her which she craved so much! "I listened to that meditation you posted on Facebook earlier. I had a lot of anxiety because of all the stuff I have to do this week...and it cleared it all away...I kept zoning in and out of sleep, but I felt so good after...'lighter' (like you said before)...and it felt like I (and the couch) were vibrating again like the last time."

My Ascension Process and Meeting My Higher Self

The concept of awakening is hard to describe. You may feel it as an expansion of your heart and soul. Perhaps it feels like you are being lifted into higher realms, like being drawn out of your body. It may be a gentle feeling of simply being more awake and aware of everything around you. Once you have awakened, the next step is the active process of Ascension. Ascension happens in waves. It is a time of rapid change, transformation, and awakening. There is no right way to ascend, we each have our own very personal experience.

Ascension work is definitely not for the faint of heart. It can be pretty profound and life-changing if you allow the process to naturally unfold and not resist the deep, sometimes unpleasant changes required to ascend. As we ascend, we leave behind old ways of thinking, acting, and BEING, letting go of all that no longer serves our highest good.

Again, once you start your awakening and Ascension process, doors open, and the right people appear at just the right times. I honestly don't even remember when or how I met the woman that would lead me to the Ascending Initiates, other than I know it was through Facebook, and somehow we were in a meditation group together online. I signed up for an Astrology reading with her; the rest is history! As I got to know her more and more; the words she used, the experiences she would talk about and the Ascended Masters that she worked with really resonated with me. Later, I discovered she was going through her Ascension with the Ascended Masters portal in New Zealand. I found myself signing up for free healings and clearings, and then signing up for a reading out of curiosity to see what initiation level I was at then. I was already a third initiate and close to being a fourth. That conscious process began for me in 2021. Ascension happens in various stages. The pace and speed at which we awaken are unique and divinely guided for each of us. It has gone fast for me.

I am at this point in June of 2023, a sixth initiate, and have cleared my karma and know this will be my last lifetime on earth. My Higher Self is continuing to become more deeply embodied in my human self, and we work together to clear and heal ourselves and others. I can verify that my Higher Self is a male. We are on the fifth ray of knowledge, truth, and healing and are a beautiful light, bright shade of green right now that I cannot put into words yet. I know when he is with me because my head and ears start buzzing out of control. I have "seen" him only once, and it was quick! He looked like a young surfer "dude" with that surfer-wavy hair. I asked him his name in my mind, and he said what I thought was "Joseph," but as I progress, I am getting more clues that lead me to believe it is not spelled or pronounced the way we say "Joseph." It is more like "Djoser," which is the name of the architect who built the first pyramid in Egypt (as I found out on my trip to Egypt). Months after returning from Egypt, I commissioned a pastel portrait to be drawn of my Higher Self by one of our fellow initiates, Shannon Guest. All she needed was a full body picture of me, what ray I am on, and if I knew if my Higher Self was male or female. When I received the picture in the mail, I could hardly believe my eyes! Sure enough, she drew a male with green eyes, a green sleeveless cutoff shirt with a tattoo and long wavy brown hair like a surfer would have. The most amazing part of all was the necklace he was wearing. I recognized it the moment I saw it. I haven't worn it in years, but I have the same necklace! It is a circular agate pendant on a leather cord. I took it as verification from him that he truly was my Higher Self if I had any doubts. Do you see how these things are not coincidental at all? They're all parts of our path, and we must go along for the ride and try to surrender and not stay stuck.

Ascension happens when you move beyond your current limitations, past the remnants of old patterns and beliefs, and into your true potential. The Ascension wave is an energetic shift that takes place on Earth. We are not going anywhere! It is not external, and there are no E.T.s landing to rescue us. Ascension is something that happens within each of us. As you continue your path, there will be shifts within you and around you to allow for new possibilities, growth, and expansion into higher versions of you. Allow this process to happen organically. Process what comes up. Allow it all to flow through you, holding on to "no-thing."

When I began embodying my Higher Self, I connected with him daily for guidance and decision-making. It made our bond strong, my trust muscle grew, and my ego and self-doubt became less and less. I will ask my Higher Self questions if I am unsure of an answer, such as, "Am I supposed to write this in my chapter of the book?" If my Higher Self is allowed to give me an answer, I will intuitively get a strong yes or no answer. That self-doubt kept creeping in in the beginning stages of getting to know and working with my Higher Self. It still does occasionally, but through the Ascending initiates, I found Carol Anne Halstead and Jan Thompson, who have their own chapters in this book. They work with dowsing rods, which I knew about but was never drawn to working with in the past. After I contacted them to do a clearing in the previous home that I lived in, they found a negative portal which was keeping me in a depressed, almost suicidal state and cleared it for me. My mood lightened, and I felt much better almost immediately. I knew I needed to learn more about working with the rods. Carol Anne's husband makes dowsing rods that Jan and Carol Anne have specifically energized to be able to work with one's Higher Self. I completed a class with Jan Thompson on how to connect my energy to that of the rods, "to connect to the embodiment of my Higher Self and gain access to the greatest teacher and healer I could ever imagine," as Jan Thompson puts it. "When you ask questions from your Sacred Heart, you connect with your Higher Self. You are no longer asking from the limitations of the mind; you are asking questions to seek the highest vibratory response and be in your truth." Working with my Higher Self in this capacity has been the greatest spiritual healing method when working with my clients. When I connect with my Higher Self and get permission from them to connect with their Higher Self, I am given guidance, clarity, and answers that are always in the highest good for everyone involved and often get us to the crux of the parts that need to be healed and resolved much quicker.

Life Coaching and the Story of Tara

Tara was referred to me because she had been holding in years of trauma and was experiencing anxiety and medical issues. Tara had no relationship at this point with anyone in her family because of the events that took place in her past. She realized that in order to move forward, she had to let her immediate family members outside of her home go. Yet they kept trying to reel her back in, and here is where she had trouble standing in her power and keeping boundaries. She is a very private person, and it wasn't until our sixth session that she even opened up to me about being an addict. She also had two failed marriages, is in a current relationship, and has two grown daughters. She finally realized she did not want to pass the trauma down and was ready to break the cycle. Tara had an "awakening." She realized there were things that happened to her as a child that she was ready to clear. Through our one-on-one coaching sessions, Tara understood that she had a pattern of not keeping her boundaries, being a people pleaser, and not giving herself any love or attention. She had become co-dependent, and we had to shift that so her daughters did not follow that same pattern. Tara was also an empath. I helped her understand that many of the emotions she was carrying around were not hers. I taught her to differentiate her emotions from others, clear her energy, and work in various situations. As we were working on these issues, she began noticing that she looked different to herself when she looked in a mirror. She looked younger and prettier! She also was no longer constipated. She had been constipated for approximately thirty years of her life. Because of my years of training in various healing modalities—including EFT (Emotional Freedom Technique) or "tapping," breath work, Reiki, chakra balancing, meditation, ancestral clearing, and spiritual mentoring—I have some tools to help anyone willing to do the work. I cannot cure anyone. I can offer advice and ideas and perform healings and clearings. I see now that the things I have gone through in my life were necessary to go through so that I can teach and help others. Learning through personal experiences creates confidence and courage, and cultivating your relationship with your Inner Teacher, the God of your understanding, and your spiritual team is a total blast! I call in my Higher Self and the Higher Self of my client and any Guides and loved ones that wish to step forward, and always ask for the information and exercises to be of the Highest Good for my client and everyone involved.

> "I reached out to Kimberley because I was stuck in a serious rut of past trauma that kept surfacing. I didn't know how to overcome this and felt I needed a knowledgeable, nonjudgmental, loving cheerleader in energy healing. Kimberley shared with me a tool chest of tools I can use to peel off those layers of trauma to reveal my true self. Kimberley is not only a gifted listener but a true teacher. She will explain in detail, show, and walk you through it. Thank you, Kimberley, for sharing your Light with me...Forever Grateful."

Your Story to Glory

For miracles to happen—for that shift in perception from Fear to Love to take place, or what I call "your story to your glory," where we're able to change our minds and transform ourselves through divine alchemy—we need to turn the words we read, hear, and consume into actual works. It requires us to take what we've heard and listened to and get a little intimate with them. I'm talking about getting intimate with the words we receive—whether those words come to us through reading, a course, a podcast, or the teachings of a mentor—and turning them into positive change for yourself through practical application.

Are you ready to turn your words into works? I am here to assist you with topics ranging from self-care and wellness, coaching, meditating, personal development and mindset work, energy healing, and abundance and alignment tools for success to help you gain exactly what you need to thrive.

Kimberley Roles, USA

https://kimberleekorner.com

YouTube: Kimberlee Korner

Instagram: @iamkjroles

Facebook: Kimberley Roles ~ Kimberlee Korner and Kids Yoga by Kim

Chapter Eight

From Birth to Rebirth: How I Became a Healer

by Lori Diebold

When you see the world from a place of love, everything changes.

Awashana

Hi, I am Lori. I am a spiritual healer, intuitive channel, teacher, and energy healer. I use my intuitive gifts to heal, inspire, and empower others. It is truly an honor for me to be a part of my client's healing journey. I had what I would call a late spiritual awakening. I had never heard of spirituality or knew anything about souls, angels, or Ascended Masters. I first became very interested in spirituality after my son passed when I was nine months pregnant at the age of thirty-eight. He was stillborn. They never did find anything medically wrong with him. I didn't understand why a baby would die. I didn't understand how or why something like this could happen. I thought death was final, and we all went into a black hole of emptiness when we died. Boy, was I wrong! I started searching for more meaning or understanding of life after death, leading me to a book with the term "Reiki healing." I felt a pull that was so strong, I had to look up Reiki healing so I could get an understanding of what it was. Once I read the description, I felt something inside me calling me to take a Reiki class. I took my first Reiki class, continued taking all levels, and became a Reiki/Master Teacher.

My path as a healer started with the Reiki classes. Then I moved on to learning many other healing modalities such as Color and Sound Healing, Channeling, Angel Therapy, RoHun Therapy, Past Life Healing, Spiritual Counseling, Animal Reiki, and the list goes on. I couldn't seem to stop taking classes, and as I did, my spiritual gifts started opening up. I started getting guidance from the Angels and the Ascended Masters, which was a huge turning point in my life. I finally felt like I was living my divine purpose and had my path laid out before me. My life started making more sense, and the significance of losing my son became apparent. I began to understand that his passing was a soul agreement between the two of us that would push me forward to my divine awakening as a spiritual healer and teacher. Instead of feeling powerless over his death, I realized that he is here with me, always leading the way and guiding me to my soul purpose, which is to help heal those that are ready to make positive changes in their lives. I am to share my knowledge with the souls awakening and needing guidance and healing. I realized that souls live on and never die, and that love will always keep the connection to your loved ones even after they cross over. They hang around us, ensuring we are ok, cheering us on.

Ascended Master Jesus once told me, "Death, to the ones left here on earth, is hard when we lose a family member, friend, or even pet, but they are going home, and there are many in heaven rejoicing to see them again. Heaven, if you will, is home; Earth is only temporary.

We are only here for a short period of time to learn our lessons, and then we go home back to the spirit world."

I am honored to bring my gifts to the world and help bring more light to those ready to shift to their true divine self.

I came upon the Alpha Imaging website and started working with Verna and Waireti, learning about the Angels and Ascended Masters, spirituality, Ascension, and how to connect with my Higher Self. At this time in my Ascension, I have passed the seventh initiation. I am on the first ray, which is the ray of God's Will and Power. My Higher Self physically appears to me with dark hair and green eyes, and she usually wears her hair up on her head with some long ringlet curls draping down on her shoulders. She told me that she may appear Asian/Indian. Her name is Awashana, which means "Sacred One." She is very caring, loving, patient, and compassionate. My Higher Self and I work with the Archangels and Ascended Masters to help bring positive healing and purpose to those who are lost and help them remember who they are. We empower them to be the divine being they came here to be. Our work is heart-based and comes from a place of divine love. We teach about self-love and help clients to learn about their own inner power and strength. My Higher Self says that she honors all of life. From animals to humans to the trees, the land, water, air, the moon, and the sun. They are all to be honored for the roles that they play on the earthly plane. They all give so much to each of us.

Healing Past Trauma with RoHun Therapy

My client, Katerina, came to me with severe fibromyalgia. The textbook meaning of fibromyalgia is a disorder characterized by widespread musculoskeletal pain accompanied by fatigue, sleep, memory, and mood issues. She was experiencing a lot of pain in and around her body. She would wake up in the morning hurting and just wanted to stay in bed. It was a struggle for her to get up and go to work every day. I was guided by my Higher Self, Angels, and the Ascended Masters to recommend the session that would benefit her the most: Rohun Therapy. This healing modality is where I identify negative thinking patterns and traumas stored in a person's energy field. Rohun Therapy is an in-depth and thorough process that taps into the unconscious regions of the mind. It releases negative thoughts and emotions that restrict and limit us and cause us to continually sabotage ourselves. It can be up to a two-hour process. Through accessing the Higher Self, Rohun effectively and lovingly releases blocked energy and hidden shadows that prevent a joyful and productive life. It works on healing the core negative emotional circumstances and past events, the traumatic and, at times, seemingly unimportant happenings that have tainted our perception and belief in ourselves. It is a deep exploration of self and self-discovery that ultimately allows you to know your true self. Rohun is a channeled therapy focusing on mental, emotional, and spiritual bodies. The session is highly interactive between the client and therapist, which helps to bring about deep and insightful change. Rohun helps clear areas of blockages and faulty perceptions to eliminate and reprogram faulty patterns to thoughts of love, wisdom, confidence, and strength.

After I explained the process and set our intentions for the healing, Katerina laid down on the healing table, and I started working at her root Chakra, which is the area around the hips, legs, and feet. I was picking up trapped emotions of unworthiness and low self-esteem. As I looked deeper into the energy in and around her chakra, I could sense fears of abandonment and rejection. I asked her about these emotions and when she first remembered having them. As we worked together, a story came to the surface of a time when her dad abused her physically and told her that she was a bad girl. This behavior from her dad continued until she was a young adult. As she started crying, trapped emotions of fear, anger, sadness, and unworthiness that were held in for most of her life surfaced. She said she felt her dad never loved or cared for her. The little girl who missed out on having a father who loved and cared for her was lying on the table. She didn't realize how this childhood memory had truly affected her throughout her adult life. We worked on giving her inner child the love, compassion, and understanding she needed and missed out on from her father. We also worked on forgiveness and understanding towards her father for the pain he put her through by getting a deeper understanding of the pain he carried all his life. I connected with his energy and recognized that he felt the same feelings that she was carrying. With this deep healing process of understanding and forgiveness, there was much release of the old hurt and pain, and she started to relax a little.

We continued moving up to her Sacral Chakra, the area right below the belly button. I saw images of her not allowing herself to have nice things and holding back on expressing herself. She admitted to not doing nice things for herself. Even when she wants flowers for her kitchen table, she will say it is too expensive. The pattern of not showing up for herself and her needs was from years of verbal abuse. We worked on the inner child that held onto these emotions and beliefs, bringing in self-love and forgiveness. As we moved on to her Solar Plexus, the area above the belly button, I felt strong trapped emotions of guilt, shame, and unworthiness. I received a vision of a woman. I asked her if there was someone in her life that made her feel unworthy. I asked her to take me back to a time when she first remembered feeling this way. She lay there crying for a few moments as she recalled when her mom told her she was a mistake and said she didn't want her. Her mom would scream at her daily, telling her she shouldn't even be there and that Katerina ruined her life by being born. She would tell her that she was ugly and shouldn't be alive. I asked her to take me back to a time when her mom yelled at her. With gentle kindness, we imagined taking her inner child by the hand and sitting down with her. Katerina told her inner child how much she loved her and assured her that she didn't do anything wrong. We went through the Rohun healing process, and Katerina said that her inner child was now happy and feeling at peace. We moved on to her heart chakra, where I saw images of her mom and dad and felt her trapped emotional pains of abandonment and feeling unlovable and unworthy. We brought back a situation where these emotions were heightened when she was a child. We worked through some self-love and healing. Katarina started to recognize that she was not to blame for her parents' actions and that they were carrying a lot of hurt and pain themselves. We moved on to her throat chakra and found trapped emotions of fear of speaking up, fear of not being heard, and fear of being judged or ridiculed. We went through a beautiful process of compassion, understanding, healing, and releasing the trapped emotions she had held onto for so long. I was starting to sense a theme here. My client was ready to move beyond her past trauma and was ready for a change in her life of self-love, self-esteem, and self-worth.

As the session unfolded, the energy around her body became stronger and brighter. The next chakra was her throat chakra. I was not surprised to feel a lot of thick, gray energy around her throat. Her voice had been restricted for most of her life. As I continued the process at her throat, I shared with her the trapped emotions I was feeling. There were heavy emotions of fear of being seen, fear of speaking up, and fear of being ridiculed. I was also picking up emotions of unworthiness and helplessness. I asked her to take me back to when she remembered feeling this way. Through tears, she said that she remembered when her mother locked her in her bedroom and didn't give her supper. Her mom said she deserved to be punished because she didn't finish washing all the dishes in the sink. Katerina cried, stating that she did all the dishes, but her mom put more in the sink after she completed her work. Feelings of being treated unfairly and beaten down were surfacing. We went through the process of love, understanding, and forgiveness. She was beginning to understand that these experiences were causing her to judge herself and feel unworthy. She believed the words that were spoken to her as a child were true. She bought into the idea that she must not be worth loving if her mom and dad thought she wasn't enough. Going through the healing process, we were able to clear these trapped emotions.

We moved on to her third eye chakra. Right away I felt and sensed heavy trapped emotions of self-judgment, low self-esteem, and fear of being judged. I was receiving images of her hiding from her mom in a closet. My client confirmed that she had hidden many times in a closet, which is where she felt at peace. We worked on her inner child, letting her feel the love she hadn't experienced. There was a lot of healing and releasing of the trapped energy she carried with her parents. There were several big releases of old, trapped emotions during the healing session.

The session was completed with me giving her the tools to continue to work on her trapped emotions and not to suppress them but to lean into them with love, compassion, and understanding for herself. Something that she didn't experience as a child, but now can do for herself. The important thing is for her to give herself what her parents couldn't give her. We are not here to judge her parents, but to know and understand that on a deeper level, these experiences that she had were for her soul's growth and to teach her about self-love and forgiveness.

I asked her to sit up when the session ended, and she said very loudly, "Oh my God!" I asked her if she was ok, and she said, "I don't feel any pain, I mean none at all! I have been hurting for three years every day and struggling to get out of bed on some days. And I am not feeling any pain." I was astonished at how all the releasing, healing, and forgiving gave her the chance to see the situations she experienced from a higher level of healing and understanding. She could let go of her circumstances and see them from a place of compassion, love, and understanding. She realized that her parents were doing the best they could, but they were in a lot of pain themselves from what they experienced throughout their lives. They were expressing their pain by lashing out at her. We all tend to sometimes lash out or treat others with anger, but in reality it is us responding to our own hurt and emotional pain that we are feeling about ourselves or what is happening in our life.

My client started to realize that she was energetically and emotionally taking on the pain of her parents and believing the negative comments as truths about her. She had an *aha* moment when she realized that her parents were carrying around a lot of pain themselves and that she was not to blame for their hurt. She felt forgiveness towards them and even some compassion! Both my client and I had tears in our eyes. What a profound healing! She learned not only how important it is to love herself, but also to forgive those who have hurt her. She now understands that her parents were her greatest teachers here on earth and that letting go and forgiving was a part of her healing process. She wasn't at all to blame for how her parents felt. They were working through their life lessons as much as she was. This was a very profound awakening for her.

Sometimes people are in our lives to help us see what we need to work on the most by how we react to them or how their words affect us. They may mirror what we feel about ourselves. What if our experiences allow us to go inward and seek answers to our emotional pain? Could it be that we are not loving ourselves enough or ignoring that part of us that felt unloved as a child? The deepest healing occurs when we tap into the hurt and hidden emotions that surface for us instead of pushing them down and avoiding them. Self-love is so important. It doesn't matter how old you are, it is never too late to learn to really love yourself by seeing your true value and worth. I spoke with my client two weeks later, and she said that she had still not experienced any pain since our session and that when she feels any sadness or anxiety, she does the inner child work shown to her during our session. What a blessing it is for me to be a part of someone's healing journey and see positive changes in their lives. And to be able to empower them with tools to help heal themselves going forward.

Healing the Past with a Past Life Healing

When I offer a Past Life Healing, I will first discuss what has been going on with my client, whether it be recent situations, patterns, behaviors, or possible issues that have been keeping them from being truly happy in their life. Once I have figured out the trapped emotions or energies of the patterns holding my client back, I will work with My Higher Self, the Ascended Masters, and Archangels. They will show me the lifetime that is most prevalent and where the patterns or behaviors originated from. I will get visions of the lifetime with details such as if the person was a male or female, ethnicity, and I will see the "story" of what happened to them then. I will see the patterns they carried from then to now. I will see the struggles, issues, and emotions that were a part of that person's story. Almost always, the story from then is very similar to what they are experiencing in this lifetime. By seeing this story, I can better understand why they are having the same issues now. We tend to bring forward similar experiences from one lifetime to the next to heal them. They are usually issues that were not dealt with in a past lifetime but are now ready to be brought to the surface to be healed. I will describe what I am seeing to my client, and we will go back to that lifetime and work on healing the trapped emotions with love, forgiveness, and compassion for the prior "self" that they were then. Through visualizations and imagination, we go back to heal what once were suppressed emotions and bring them to a deeper awareness and understanding.

My client, Joan, sought my services because she was feeling hopeless with anger, sadness, and powerlessness. She said that she felt a lot of heaviness in her chest. Once the session started, she shared how she had been feeling and the struggles that she was having in her life. When I connected with her energy, I sensed a fear of loss, being let down, and losing her faith. I asked her about this, and she explained that she had lost a child during a miscarriage six months before our appointment. Joan had lost hope about ever getting pregnant again.

I was shown a past lifetime where Joanh had lost her husband and then a child shortly after. Together, through a brief process, we went back to that time. Joan had an opportunity to sit with this woman whom she was in this past lifetime. When I asked her what emotions were coming up, she said that she sensed this woman's sadness, pain, anger, hopelessness, and distrust. She saw that she had lost her faith and had given up hope.

I was shown an image of her shaking her fist at the heavens saying, "Why, why, why?" and blaming God. She also blamed herself and asked what she did wrong to deserve this heartache.

She decided to shut down in that lifetime after losing her husband and baby. She thought that after losing her husband, she would at least have a part of him as she was pregnant with his child. But once her baby died, she totally shut down and wanted to give up on life. We went through the healing process where she expressed love, compassion, and understanding to this prior self. I was shown that this woman in her past life had two children in the other room. When I shared this with Joan, it brought a sense of peace to her. Spirit spoke through me, explaining to this woman that it was time to live for the other two children that needed her desperately. She was told that she is stronger than she can imagine and not to give up on herself. This was a soul contract between her and her husband. Her husband is eternal and will always be with her, watching over her. She was guided not to blame herself, but to see the power that she has within her.

Something beautiful happened as the soul of her husband from that lifetime appeared and said that he loved her and her living children. That he still needed her, and for her to live for him. He was sorry that he left early, but he knew they would be together again. He knew that he would have a short lifetime. No one was to blame. This was a soul lesson for her to forgive herself, move forward in her power, and rise above guilt and blame. After this healing took place, I was shown that in that lifetime she moved on to help others with losses. She used her experience to help others. I had Joan look into the eyes of her prior self and see her qualities and strengths. She said that she felt her courage and beautiful heart and how this past self was willing to help others by drawing from her experiences. We took her to the end of that life, where we could see that she had remarried, found love again, and still had her beautiful children—who love her dearly—by her side. We observed that she left this body with no regrets, but with gratitude and grace for her life. There were no signs of anger, powerlessness, or loss of hope. She had lived out her days in joy and service. You could see a shift in Joan after this powerful experience. She now understands why she was struggling with these emotions and understood the lessons that she came here to learn.

It is true that we can go back to a past lifetime and heal a part of us, having it positively affect our lives from the past and today. After the session was over, she sent me a testimonial. This is what she shared with me:

> "The healing itself was beyond anything I had expected. The process wasn't complicated or

> arduous at all. It was so fascinating to just walk into one of my previous lives and perform the healing right there. Not only did I feel the healing emotionally, but I also actually felt the healing physically. At the end of my session, I felt that a weight had been lifted from my chest, and it still feels that way today, and it has been over a month. Lori received insights and information through her intuitive abilities, which were indescribably valuable. This session was like spiritual empowerment coaching for me. I will forever be grateful to you and your healing team for the transformation I have experienced."

Past Life Healing: How Fears Can Repeat Lifetime after Lifetime

Another client, Susan, came to me for a Past Life Healing session. She was carrying a lot of fears. She is a spiritual healer with many gifts to share with others but is afraid to get herself out there. Once we discussed what had been going on with her, we were ready to start the session.

When I connected with her energy, I was immediately drawn to her throat chakra, where there were trapped emotions of fear of speaking her truth and fear of being judged by others when speaking. She confirmed that this had been holding her back her whole life. I was also immediately drawn to her heart by my spirit team of healers. I was picking up trapped emotions of being hurt by others and not being able to trust others. Susan confirmed that she does carry these emotions. Next, I was taken to her third eye chakra, where I picked up patterns of fear, of being judged by others, self-judgment, and abandonment of self by holding back self-expression. Her solar plexus was lighting up for me, which meant that there were some trapped emotions there as well. Here I picked up some guilt and shame and showed that she was feeling guilt and shame for holding herself back from being the healer she came here to be. There was a form of duality where she wanted to get herself out there and help others, but the fear was holding her back. I was shown by my spirit guides that the guilt and shame were coming from not moving forward with her soul's plan of self-expression and sharing her knowledge with others. I was drawn to another place with some trapped emotions on her body. It was her root chakra, which is the area from around the hips down to the feet. I was finding some fear of moving forward.

I connected with my healing team and asked them to take me back to a lifetime when she was affected most by these stuck patterns of behavior. I was shown a lifetime where she was a psychic and medium. The vision became clearer when I was taken to her childhood, where she just "knew things." She would tell friends at school that she knew what they were thinking of doing for their birthday party, or she would tell them things that no one else knew. It would scare the children, and they would tell their parents and teachers. She soon became an outcast, and no one wanted to be around her because she was different. She was an innocent child who didn't know any better and was excited to share what she knew with others, but soon she became ashamed of her gifts as she was called names and made fun of for not being like everyone else. Eventually, her parents told her not to share her psychic gifts with anyone. She didn't even feel accepted by her parents. This created trapped emotions of inability to express herself or be herself. She had to hide who she truly was. She felt terribly ashamed of her gifts and learned to suppress her emotions.

Susan stopped me at this point and said that the lifetime I was seeing was so similar to this lifetime, that it was almost as if I was discussing experiences that she had been through in this life. Susan admitted that when she was a child, she had the ability just to know things about others and their true intentions. Her parents would tell her that what she was doing was not nice and not to share her "know-ings" or truth with others.

Eventually, in that past lifetime, word got around about her and the work that she was doing. She felt the need to hide, but those who needed help would find or seek her out. One day she heard that some people in her town wanted to find her and threatened her life. She felt fearful for her life. She went into hiding. Her calling then was to help others just like in this lifetime and to serve humanity. She became depressed and held onto a lot of fear and self-judgment. She was not able to express herself fully as to who she was. She brought these exact patterns to this lifetime to understand and heal. We continued working in the past, as I was shown images in my mind of her getting older and going off on her own and learning to use her gifts to help others and make money since she needed money to live. I was shown that during that lifetime she was very loving and heart-centered. She loved helping others. She changed many lives in that lifetime. She brought peace and hope to others, which is what she is here to do in this lifetime.

Susan explained to me that this all made so much sense because she knew things about a family member and threatened to tell everyone. The family member threatened her life and her children's lives this lifetime if she said anything. You can see the parallel lifetimes. She said that she now sees the similarity between both lifetimes: if she speaks her truth, she may receive death threats or feel threatened by others. She lives in fear this lifetime as well. She feels that she must hide and is not safe.

I was so grateful that spirit brought me to a lifetime of Susan's that mirrored this. It was time to work on healing and understanding why Susan brought these patterns forward. With the help of my guides, we gently and safely took Susan back through a brief process that spirit has taught me. We found her former self in a cave in a fearful state and filled with sadness. There were trapped emotions of guilt and shame by how others saw her. Also, she feared being seen and not accepted for who she was.

Through the healing process offered by my Higher Self, the Angels and Ascended Masters offered love, compassion, and understanding to this "former self." Susan's former self received and accepted the healing on a deep soul level. We worked on forgiveness, understanding, and compassion for those that put her in this situation in that lifetime. I was shown that some people who accused her of wrongdoings were her family in this lifetime. They are all here to work on the karma that was created and to learn the lessons that were not learned back then. Spirit guides spoke through me, saying that these souls were brought to her in that lifetime for her soul to expand and grow. She was to remember who she was as a soul and to love and accept herself for who she was, which was a guiding light for others. It was also explained to her that she has come to earth in other lifetimes, played a role reversal, and treated her family similarly. Our soul wants us to experience both the victim and perpetrator in different lifetimes with our soul family.

Lastly, she was shown the "love" that these souls who were against her in both the past and current lifetime all have on a deep soul level for her and each other. All there is is love when they are on the other side of the veil, and they will have it once again when they shed their human bodies and transition back to a pure conscious soul. Once they come through the veil on earth, they forget the soul contracts or "roles" that they have agreed to play in this lifetime, or the lessons that they are here to learn together. Once the healing took place, Susan could forgive them and let go of the pain they caused. She learned that true forgiveness from the heart will set her free from the cords that have been created from that lifetime and this lifetime. Forgiveness is one of the lessons that she is here to learn. She became more aware of how people carry fear and pain from their own insecurities and feelings of powerlessness. Mother Mary, Jesus, and White Tara stepped forward to help her with this healing. It was so beautiful to witness this powerful healing as it took place. It feels like a small miracle each time I see the change that can occur when we go back and heal the past with love and compassion. We also gain a new perspective and can heal on a deeper level.

A week after her session, Susan sent me this note:

> "Lori, you do the most beautiful work – God's work of healing the heart! I am profoundly grateful, and my life is forever improved. Your gifts helped mend a broken heart with pure light and love. Your generous nature and gentle approach are remarkable. Words do not suffice."

Lori Diebold, USA

The Healing Heart

Website: www.thehealingheart.love

Instagram: @thehealingheart.love

Chapter Nine

From Chaos to Unconditional Love

by
Heather Corinne Lang

When we embrace and express unconditional love in all our endeavors and relationships, we help others heal.

-Oleianya (O-lay-an-ya)

My Healing and Spiritual Path

Throughout my life, others have expressed to me that they always feel "better" around me. They feel more balanced and peaceful; they feel happier and calmer. I found many of these individuals would come to me when experiencing issues in any given area of their lives. Co-workers would come to my desk and sit down and start sharing what troubles they were having outside of work, ask me to help them interpret a dream they had, or get information on the type of foods I eat because they wanted to get healthier. This has been a pattern for the better part of the past twenty years of my life. Friends, family, and others have come to me naturally to ask me about something to help them. I have been told how much I have helped someone through my blog or social media posts. Even now, my co-workers and the customers who have come to know me ask me about astrology, health and wellness, and what I do to stay looking so young. My soul journey has included both physical and metaphysical aspects, as I have learned so much about so many different areas of health and wellness. I've always loved getting astrology and Tarot readings, talking to psychics and intuitives, and learning about the spiritual world. It just took me a while to learn that I loved it because I was meant to do something like it.

Two Families and Two Belief Systems

I grew up in the Catholic religion on my mother's side. We went to church nearly every Sunday and had classes on Monday nights. We were baptized and had Confirmation. I was married in the Catholic Church. This religion was part of my belief system.

My father's side, which included my Nana, was more metaphysical and spiritual. This was common to that side and became part of my belief system. They blended for me as I felt they both made sense, so they are both a big part of my journey and I am thankful to both sides of my family. But it was Nana who started my understanding and love of the spiritual and metaphysical world.

Nana would go to church, but the Catholic faith wasn't important to her. She just liked the energy she felt when she needed it. She would come with us on Christmas Eve and Easter. But she was also very interested in Tarot and card readings, psychic readings, astrology, past lives, and much more. I remember she was always talking about supplements and vitamins as part of her health and wellness. And, of course, she took my sister and me to our first reader, who read cards and tea leaves! Her name was Ms. Jo. I recall Ms. Jo telling me a lot of things, but what stuck with me the most was her telling me that I would be helping a lot of people. At the time, she suggested it could be through being a doctor, counselor, or psychiatrist. While those fields were interesting, back then I wasn't "feeling it." I wasn't sure that was what I wanted to be. I now find it interesting that she was naming these mainstream careers. Because a possibility was planted in my mind, I investigated them and even took a psychology course in college. I found it fascinating, but I didn't want to major in it or become a psychologist or psychiatrist. I also knew I couldn't stomach going through med school!

I was led to energy work, life guidance, astrology, crystals, essential oils, and all things metaphysical after college, but I still remembered my first reading with Ms. Jo and how it was normal for Nana to say things like, "Oh, that's because of your Aquarius cusp!" Or she would start a story with, "You, your father, and I were in a past life together in which we..." It captured my attention unlike anything else. As I grew up, the more I delved into these alternative metaphysical beliefs and practices, the more I wanted to learn about them. I was and still am fascinated by anything new and different.

It is a good time to note that when I was in grade school, I loved magic! My two favorite TV shows to watch were, "Bewitched" and "I Dream of Jeannie." I used to role-play with my sister, acting as if I was Samantha or Jeannie. Back then, I was already showing signs of what I wanted to do—magically (energetically) help others. And I have come to believe we are magical, energetic, manifesting spiritual beings. We must remember and re-learn how to do magic through our actions, words, and thoughts.

In addition to the metaphysical, I have always been interested in other individuals' belief systems, cultures, and lifestyles. One of my best friends in high school was from India, and she told me so much about their beliefs and religion. I went to her wedding, which was such a great time and a wondrous learning experience. I also enjoyed learning about Native American beliefs and cultures later in life from another friend. She had books about symbolism through animals. I now have that same book! I began learning about Native American symbolism, totem animals, animal spirit guides, and more. Again, it fascinated me. The more I could learn, the happier I became with this new knowledge.

When I was about thirty years old, my sister and I went to see another card reader, a lovely Puerto Rican guy. His name is Ernesto. He is Wiccan and has taught me quite a bit about that belief system and about Puerto Rican beliefs. I'm happy to say I'm still friends with him, and we continue to learn from each other. I love that Wicca is about nature, like Native American beliefs. I have been called a tree-hugger at times! Anyway, he was the one who first taught me about crystals. The first one was Lapis Lazuli to help me connect my mind and heart. I tend to overanalyze things, and this did help me a lot. I found I loved working with crystal energy and still do to this day. I have often given my clients certain crystals to hold during their sessions and/or told them which one(s) could help them at this time and how to use them. Ernesto is also the first person I knew to speak Light Language. He once told me that he saw me moving my hands around in the air like I was making symbols or something. We later discovered I was drawing Light Language over my clients to assist in their healing. Since then, I still do this over some clients, and at times I have spoken a few Light Language phrases in sessions and when interacting with him.

I have always been able to see and accept the multiple ways people view the world; that there are so many various concepts and beliefs. I accept others, knowing their path isn't necessarily the one I am on, nor should it be. Therefore it feels like I attract many different types of people, although we always find common ground or a similar experience. I have also had a few longer-term intimate relationships, which definitely taught me a lot! Many of my clients come to me with relationship issues and injuries, needing some direction in life. Being open to many different types of people, cultures, beliefs, and ways of being has helped me be more open-minded and open-hearted, which attracts people and is part of unconditional love.

Energetically, our bodies manifest what we need to work on, and I have had issues with my spinal alignment. It was in my late twenties when I went to my first chiropractor. He told me my neck was straight and normally should be curved forward. He told me I had one vertebra that was sunken in towards the top of my shoulders and that my spine curved near my heart, which is why my hips were out of alignment. During my energy work on myself over the past ten years, the things I have worked on the most are relationships. It makes sense that my spine wasn't in alignment near my heart. And I have had trouble speaking my truth, at times speaking it only to be told I was wrong. Since speaking my truth over many lifetimes led to incarceration, being outcast, and/or killed, I can see why my neck was ramrod straight. I did not have the flexibility to speak my truth.

Yoga was My Savior

I was married for about five-and-a-half years to someone with addiction issues. I ended up paying for our home, groceries, and bills. We had to sell the condo and move in with his parents after we did an intervention. He agreed to go to a halfway house to get help. I went to Al-Anon for a while, which I enjoyed, as it helped teach me quite a bit about addictions, those with them, and how to love through detachment. I did go to a professional counselor at the time, as did he, yet the marriage did not last. I am grateful for that time since Al-Anon and counseling helped me in many ways. Much of what I learned can be applied to all facets of different life issues. I've been divorced for about nineteen years now. However, I've had a few other relationships, reinforcing things I needed to learn about boundaries, finances, and other relationship issues. It seemed I was dating the same type of man I had married. I was repeating a pattern I needed to clear to help myself heal. Men who were attracted to me used me in some way financially and then ended up leaving or hurting me in the end. Lots of chaos, drama, and imbalanced energy seemed to keep showing up in each relationship a little more heavily and intensely each time, which was all unsettling. However, the traumatic experience with my ex-husband was pivotal in my healing journey, giving me some tools to deal with the other two relationships and thus heal and grow. After the third relationship ended about seven years ago, I decided to be really focused on dealing with the pattern and healing myself so I could let it all go.

One day after my ex-husband and I had moved into his parents' home, my former mother-in-law suggested I attend yoga with her to help with the stress her son was causing us both. I loved it! Yoga was my sanctuary back then. I learned as much as possible about it through yoga teachers, magazines, and whatever else I could find. I was able to find my inner peace during times of chaos when my ex-husband still wasn't home by 3 am. I was able to create more balance and calm in my life. I went to classes a few times per week and practiced in the morning and at night with recordings when I wasn't in class. I found friends in class and camaraderie with many of them. I still think fondly about my first teacher and how much I learned from her on many different levels. Yoga saved me back then, and I continued practicing for a while, even leading classes for several years. Between yoga, Al-Anon, counseling, and self-help books, I was finding my way onto my path of health and wellness and all that it entails.

Up Next, Reiki

Because I did yoga and understood chakras, a friend of mine who had learned Reiki—and decided she wanted to teach it to others—asked if I would be one of her test students. I had never heard of Reiki, but her description of it sounded right up my alley. Of course, I agreed, as I was craving something new with more knowledge and wisdom. I had just returned from a somewhat unsettling time in a different state with my second chaotic relationship and could use a focus. I was hooked at the first class! I felt right at home re-learning about the chakras and about the different Ascended Masters, Angels, and Archangels. I was learning what energy work could do and how to do it. When I received the first attunement, I was absolutely amazed at what I felt. I'd never experienced something like that. My entire neck and upper back heated up, and I felt intensely uplifted and full of potent energy! My hands started to tingle and become warm. I felt like I was glowing. Each attunement after that was similar but seemed to add another layer. Interestingly, whenever I receive energy work from someone else, my neck and back heat up. When I send energy, I can feel it in my hands and areas of my body where the client needs energy or something released and cleared.

I loved learning something that could help others, because even as a teenager I knew I was meant to do so. The way had just not presented itself yet. For a while, I thought maybe it was yoga, but that didn't happen. I was initially trained in Practical Reiki, an intention-based form. I learned other healing techniques from other energy workers, such as vibrational and color energy, White Light Reiki, crystal energies, and some Native American healing energy. My style seems to be a blend of all I have learned in this lifetime and other lifetimes. I discovered during my journey that I have had many lives as some type of healer. I feel like this is the lifetime where all I have learned is culminating in helping others in all different ways depending on their belief systems and what they are attracted to at the time.

While each session I have is different, they are all very powerful, and I am still amazed at what happens. My sessions are more interactive, as the client will tell me about an incident or experience that has troubled them. But sometimes the client is just there to get a boost of energy, relax, and rejuvenate. Most often, my sessions offer intuitive guidance, knowledge, and wisdom sharing. The messages range from what crystal can help the client to how they may want to change their diet, or how to interact in certain situations. At times their ancestors and current spirit guides—as well as spirit, totem, or messenger animals—come through for assistance and support. I also learned a lot about essential oils as part of my love of health and wellness, and at times a message comes through about which essential oil can help, or which type of herb or plant medicine can help them.

About eight years ago, five of us met and taught each other what we knew metaphysically. I recall one of the girls saying to me, "You are the most claircognizant of all of us." I thought this was a lovely compliment considering our group of girls at the time! We then decided to offer energy sessions and provide psychic messages. This led to learning even more from each other and later to a point where only three of us could offer these sessions. This turned into just me and one other gal for a few years. (It ended due to the pandemic because at that time no one wanted to come.) We helped many clients in many ways, and people loved coming to these sessions. They also taught me more about the style of energy work that came naturally to me. I became even more intuitive and sensitive, feeling ancestors, spirit guides, totem animals, Angels, Archangels, and Ascended Masters.

My Ascension Journey

I started my Ascension journey in December 2018 when I received my first reading from the Alpha Imaging website. There is wonderful information on their website that helped me and made a lot of sense to me, especially information about my Ascension ray. I had incarnated on the fourth ray of harmony through conflict. This explained why I had so many challenging learning experiences with relationships. They weren't always my intimate ones. Sometimes they were with friends. I recall befriending a girl when I was in grade school, and after I included another girl, we became a trio. But after a few months, these girls bullied me and told me they didn't want me around anymore. That was my first taste of conflict and not understanding why others could be so mean. It probably started my journey of wanting to learn about other people, as I had become the underdog and found I could relate better to them. They were different, unique, and interesting. It also helped explain why I became a people pleaser and a chameleon. I just wanted to fit in and not upset anyone because I didn't like being bullied. I didn't want to hurt people either, as I had been hurt. But it was the most wonderful thing to happen, since it put me on the trajectory that has become my life and learning to love others no matter what our differences, opinions, beliefs, or understandings about life are.

At this writing, I have passed the seventh initiation with my Higher Self completely embodied. My Higher Self is on the third ray of unconditional love. I had been confused about which ray I was on for months because I kept seeing a pink color that was more of the Goddess Ray ruby color, but for some reason that just didn't seem entirely right. One day while driving to work, I asked my Higher Self specifically to give me a sign, symbol, or image and to make it very clear. About halfway to work, the word "Oleander" randomly popped into my mind. After work I looked it up to discover it was all about love. This flowering plant is about all types of love, even love which can be "poisonous," like obsessions, attachments, or infatuation, and even love which can be controlling or manipulating in some way. This type of love gives us great lessons through the challenge, even if we are unaware of it then. It feels like a blending of my old Ascension ray with my Higher Self's Ascension ray! I had the third ray of unconditional love as my mental ray, so I was familiar with it already. I had worked with Kuan Yin, who was the Ascended

Master on this ray. I recall having an energy healing session with someone who had seen that Kuan Yin was with me and had entered my heart chakra.

My other rays played integral parts in my life story and helped me understand my life and what I needed to work on, heal from, and let go. My other rays included: the second ray of wisdom, joy, and lightness of being with Ascended Master Jesus as my Life Ray. This also explains a lot about my life and my need to include joy in everything I do, gain wisdom, and have lightness all the time, as we also experience non-light times for our lessons and growth.

With the sixth ray of the goddess and devotion as my emotional ray, I needed to learn to embrace my inner goddess as part of my emotional ray and devote energy to myself, my inner goddess, and my Higher Self. Pallas Athena was the Ascended Master who helped me here. I had always been attracted to Pallas Athena, so it was very interesting that she was with me on this ray.

The first ray of God's Will and Power was my physical ray with St. John the Baptist. This was learning about humbling myself and knowing that a power greater than me can help me physically! This also includes the power of meditation, since we can ask (pray) all we want, but we also must learn to listen to our inner guidance while taking action on what we desire to create and manifest.

Back to my Higher Self, who appears to me in two main ways. She shows herself as a Native American with black hair (sometimes in two braids, other times down her back). She has blue eyes, and she wears a pink stone in the middle of a band made of gold around her head. She tends to wear both a "buckskin" outfit and, at times, is dressed in a white and pink shimmering gown. Most of the time she appears as pure love energy with many different types of pink, yet her main color is dark pink, like ruby pink or darker pink tourmaline.

Interestingly, I was drawn to the color pink while I was working on my Ascension, and I thought maybe it was because of Kuan Yin, who was my Master for my mental ray. Before I knew my Higher Self, I would smell a lovely light flowery scent, like the oleander flower, and this was how my Higher Self got my attention and let me know she was with me. And her name is Oleianya (pronounced as *O-lay-an-ya*)!

While I have learned to master the fourth ray of harmony through conflict, and I still experience it occasionally, I am now learning to embody the third ray of unconditional love with my Higher Self. Therefore, when I am not feeling very harmonious in a space or relationship, I can find my way back through all my knowledge coupled with unconditional love.

Intuitive Energy Healing Sessions

My sessions are very client-focused and specific to what the client needs. I have clients who just want to be rejuvenated and revitalized. I have others who want peace, harmony, and calming energy. I have some who come for physical pain. I have others who come for mental clarity. Others are experiencing emotional turmoil. Many clients have issues with relationships, careers, finances, and more. Many clients come back because prior sessions helped them and now they need help with another issue. Some come because they simply love how they feel for weeks after the sessions. Sometimes the client doesn't even realize what they need until it materializes during the session, such as past life issues or other reasons why they aren't feeling "right."

I Rolled My Three-Wheeler!

I have a friend who attended yoga sessions with me when I worked in an office. After I left that company, she rolled her three-wheeler. She had heard me talk about Reiki but had never tried it. She finally came to me weeks after her accident. The doctors just told her to keep taking ibuprofen and to rest. She said it had been six weeks, and she still was in a lot of pain and decided to finally give Reiki a try because she trusted me from yoga. When she walked in, I could see she was struggling as she couldn't stand completely straight and was limping a bit. We gently eased her onto the Reiki table and made her comfortable with a pillow and bolster. She had a half-hour session. After the session, I did a few assisted yoga stretches with her. She exclaimed that she felt 80 percent better and practically jumped off the table! She had three more sessions to help with that accident. When she left after the last session, she said she felt 100 percent better. She still comes occasionally for general things, like a refresh or to de-stress. And as a bonus, she mentioned to me that her ribs and hip haven't bothered her all these years later since those initial Reiki sessions.

I Fell Down the Stairs!

A lady from a different state contacted me one day. She had seen my social media posts and those about Reiki, so she visited my website. She thought Reiki could possibly help her and wanted to give it a try. Her body hurt from injuries, and she was having issues mentally. After her session, she said she felt better and would schedule another one. She was also going to schedule a doctor's visit, as intuitively I sensed she had a fracture near the side of her head that hurt, near her temple. She contacted me after the doctor's appointment, and sure enough she had a fracture. So in the next couple of sessions we worked on helping her body heal the fracture, plus the other injuries. She told me she felt so much healing energy within her and felt so much better after the sessions. She had more sessions for different reasons, plus some readings. She is a lovely friend now and a repeat client.

Interesting, I'd Like to Try It!

Several years ago, a co-worker asked me to talk about Reiki to their single-parent group. I enjoyed providing them with information, and one person said she'd heard about it, while another said she had tried it. One man handed me his card and said, "This is interesting, I'd like to try it, so please contact me." After his first session, he was hooked. He had been divorced for a long time, and his children weren't really in his life. He came monthly (and still does as my longest client of about ten years) and enjoyed the spiritual messages, visits from ancestors, and the general calm he felt after the sessions. He also enjoyed how the energy made his sore joints, neck, and shoulders feel afterwards. His desk job had been taking a toll on his physical body. It was really an honor to see his transition over time. He became more intuitive over the years and now tells me what's happening, including dreams he has and the energy he feels. He has a better relationship with himself and has been talking to his daughter again. I love when clients are able to heal and find self-love. To me this is the number one thing to work on with my clients! Having the best relationship we can with ourselves, because when we learn to love ourselves unconditionally, we will attract others who love us in the same way.

I Am Not Getting Along with My Daughter!

A man came for energy work, and it turned out he was having issues with his daughter, which stemmed from his current intimate relationship with a woman and her daughter. During the session, past lives came up for each of these relationships for releasing and healing. I then focused on healing the energetic cords between himself and his daughter, plus the two new relationships. He came several times, and we worked on other past lives in which he had experienced similar issues. I recall a beautiful scene the guides showed me at his last session in which his daughter was in a lovely open sunny field of wildflowers, and she was dancing as a much younger child. The message was that she felt healed, happier, and better through these sessions. He was elated at this, and last I heard, all of them were getting along very well.

My Mom is in the Hospital!

A client of mine contacted me to see if I would visit her mom in the hospital and give her Reiki. I of course complied! I went a few times. Her mom was suffering and was not getting better from a horrible disease. The first time I went, her mom wasn't very aware and was in quite a bit of pain, so she kept moving around, attempting to get comfortable. I sat by her bed, put my hands towards her, and simply let the energy flow. After about five minutes, her mom started to calm down and wasn't moving around much. I could sense she was feeling more comfortable. I continued to send energy for about a half hour. After the session, her mom opened her eyes and looked at me. My friend introduced me, and her mom smiled at me. She motioned me over to the bed to get closer to her. She put her hand lovingly on my face. I could feel her gratitude through the energy. It was both a humbling and lovely experience. My heart swelled with her love and gratitude. Later, my friend said her mom told her how much better she felt after my visit. I went two more times. The second time, her mom hugged me and thanked me for coming. My friend said her mom could feel the energy and really enjoyed it. She said her mom was very thankful and felt better after my visit. The third time, she touched my face again after I was finished, as if she was saying goodbye. She passed away a few days later. My friend said I had given her mom so much comfort, peace, and calm during her final weeks, and both she and her mom were very grateful. It was I who was grateful and honored to be able to offer the energy and be a part of her transition to the next world.

Unconditional Love Heals

With all these clients, I have found that my acceptance of all different ways of living, believing, being, and relating has really helped me help others heal themselves. And now, with my Higher Self, the unconditional love pours forth in my sessions and even interactions with others. I currently work in a very busy and physically demanding job in a restaurant. My Higher Self loves going to "work," AKA the restaurant. I can feel her enthusiasm at being able to help those we come into contact with, whether they are customers, co-workers, or suppliers. The place has become more serene with her presence. When others are upset, she sends them love. I don't know everything she is doing for others, but she certainly has kept me in a more loving and harmonious state in a place that can be very chaotic. She loves being around my friends and family. While I am not sure yet what she is doing, I do know she is surrounding me, my clients, my family, my friends, and those I am generally around in a huge energetic blanket of unconditional love. And, as she likes to say, "Unconditional love heals."

Heather Corinne Lang, USA

Website: www.NamasteRays.com

Facebook: https://www.facebook.com/heather.lang.19

Instagram: https://www.instagram.com/heatherclang/

Chapter 10

Turning the Old into Gold

By Tammy Manzo

You have the ability to change and rearrange whatever you want in your life. That is your Divine right as a human being doing your work on the earth plane. Exercise this Divine right boldly to create those things you do want and alchemize (change) those things that you don't want.

-Will-IAM

There was an energy out in the world in the summer of 2009 that woke a lot of souls up. I was one of those souls. Many people I know also woke up at that time. If this was you or anybody you know, you may be interested in learning why that happened and what brought it about. And don't worry if you were too young to wake up at that time; there was also another great awakening in the spring of 2022. Those of us who were already awakened were also boosted on our spiritual paths at that time.

It all has to do with energy.

Perhaps you already know that we are souls in a body learning to master the energies on planet Earth. I believe our souls have come here with a blueprint, a rough outline of how we will create our journeys. There are certain things we are here to complete, certain things we are here to help others with, and certain things we will learn that are new. This is a journey of a thousand-petal lotus flower, and each petal will unfold in its time—at the right time, not a minute before and not a minute later. The right time is always happening. One can see this timing in an astrology chart.

The Power of Astrology

Some people don't believe in astrology, and I can understand why. There is a lot of misinformation, some of which can be downright hurtful, besides being incorrect. Some forms of astrology are full of gloom and doom, such as the idea of "being born under a bad star." This attitude leaves no room for free will. This is not the astrology that my Higher Self and I work with. We work with energy. We look at astrology as pure energy. The planets are different energies, and the twelve astrology signs are the vibrations (or filters) that each of these energies can express. I believe that our souls take turns over all our past lifetimes, experiencing what life is like as each of the different sun and moon signs, and every other planet in all the different signs. I read somewhere that there are approximately 350,000 different possible combinations of planets and signs that an astrology chart could have. The chance of you and someone else having an identical astrology chart is 350,000 to 1. Even twins born at slightly different times could have different charts. Just six minutes between their births could create a big difference. You can see how unique we are. This is just amazing!

Not only do we have combinations of energy in our charts, but there is energy in the cosmos that helps us to grow and learn. There are new and full moons, eclipses, and the movement of the planets themselves, which brings us the energy that we are learning to master. We are here to learn, experience, create, and manifest our lives with free will within the framework of the energies we have available to us.

And you can see all of this in your astrology chart.

You can see the timing and cycles of energy there. This is true of us individually and as a collective. We, as humans, work with energy together and in our own ways, in our own lives, each on our different paths.

Once in a while, there is a combination of energy out in the world that is unique and special and opens a door of possibilities. It creates a new timeline, and if it aligns with our soul's blueprint, we will connect to it, and things will start to happen quickly. This is what happened in the summer of 2009.

Without being too technical, this was the conjunction of Neptune, Jupiter, and Chiron. Neptune is the soul; Jupiter brings the blessing, expansion, and opportunities; and Chiron is the archetype of the wounded healer. I see this as the souls who were healers in other lives—and intended to become healers again—stepping onto this timeline. Things happened rapidly from there.

Everybody's journey is different, but for me it was all about working with energy and vibration of all kinds. My specific orientation is changing situations and changing lives, while others might choose to create or manifest.

It was a crazy crash course for sure. I felt like I was being downloaded all the time with information and guidance on what to do and study next. And I felt like I was pushed really hard to hurry, hurry, hurry! Go, baby, go!

Tarot, Reiki, and Practical Reiki

The first thing I learned was tarot. I had always gone to readers, and I was very interested in the pictures on the cards and wondered what they meant. In 2009, I found a deck of tarot cards at Goodwill which I recognized as the Universe's store. The Universe left things for me there. At the time I was a seller on eBay, which I really enjoyed because I have a marketing degree, and I used to be in advertising sales for a newspaper. I had the knack of finding these odd bits and bobs at the Goodwill that people would pay money for. (Once, I sold a vintage board game for $92. I also found a Louis Vuitton wallet. Not sure if it's authentic, but I love it anyway.)

Oddly enough—but not really odd, of course—I tried to sell those tarot cards, but nobody wanted them. That was a sign! I would just use them myself. Tarot really helps to open up one's intuition and spiritual gifts and abilities, and that was a fun and easy way to start on the path. And I was learning things about myself and my life through the messages of the cards.

The next thing that came was Reiki. It was brought to me by my spirit guides and angels. I was standing in the library aisle where all the astrology and metaphysical content was shelved. I pulled out a book, and another book fell out with it. It was about Reiki, which I had never heard of. I was already quickly following signs, so I took the book home. Within less than an hour of reading it, I knew I wanted to do it. It took all summer searching online to find somebody that taught Reiki in Ohio.

Finally, I learned Usui Reiki in September 2009. I remember receiving my first energy attunement when the teacher was drawing symbols on my lower spine. It felt like magnetic energy as if something was being pulled out, but also being put in. I asked my friend if she felt that during her attunement, and she said, "No." That was when I knew that something special had happened, just for me.

Many years later, being able to feel energy through my body is a spiritual gift that just keeps getting stronger and stronger. I can feel energy across time zones and past lives. I started to find my past lives a few years ago by accident. I would be reading about a person or place, or watching a television show or movie, and if this were something from a past life of mine, I would feel strong energy coming down through my crown. Sometimes I would also get goosebumps or shivers.

Now this ability has expanded to not only knowing my own past lives, but I can pick up on people that I knew in those lives. I can find my children and husbands and wives from that lifetime. Now I need to ask, "Is this me or a relative or friend of mine?"

I can also find the past lives of people in astrology readings. If they have been with me in a past life that I already know about, it will come up in the reading. Then I say, "Oh, I knew you from this lifetime!" At first I was shy about this because I didn't want people to think I was crazy, and I didn't want to scare them off. So far, everybody has been receptive to hearing this information. I have a strong lifetime as one of America's founding fathers, and that's one of the timelines that attracts the most past life connections for me. Several past-life founding fathers have shown up for readings. One of these people and I message each other to say, "Happy July 4th!" every year. It is surreal but so, so amazing.

That brings us to astrology. I have always studied it, from many past lives to the current lifetime, even before there was the internet. I remember being about twelve years old and having an astrology book and getting caught by my father with it. We were strict Catholics, and in the 1970s it was not accepted in that religion. It still may not be accepted. If you have read our earlier book, *Modern Ascension*, you may remember my chapter about breaking away from the religion that I loved so much because it didn't give me the space to work with astrology, past lives, tarot, and energy healing.

I still have no idea how I would have obtained the astrology book. I was also burning incense in my room and have no idea how I would have gotten that either. But I have always been a person who will go against the status quo, break some outdated rules, push the boundaries, and bust up some old stuck energy. I do this for myself first, and I am always doing it. It's like blazing a trail that my clients can follow. I love nothing better than pushing the envelope farther and farther to see what is possible. I am an observer and a participant, always trying new things.

In 2012, I learned Practical Reiki. This was a system I was resisting until my spirit guides and angels told me I needed to learn it. I still teach Practical Reiki today. This system of Reiki does not use Japanese symbols and structured hand positions, but rather encourages you to use your intuitive senses. It makes them stronger as well. The energy is directed through command statements rather than the symbols, and so allows one the space to create their own healing sessions. It is very empowering. I've taught about fifty people so far, and it's been wonderful. When I was a young child, I wanted to be a teacher, and I used to make up school lessons, tests, and quizzes for fun during summer vacations. I spent years volunteering at my son's schools when he was younger as well. All good practice for what was to come!

In case you have never heard of Reiki, or are not sure what it is and what it can do, here is a very basic description. Again, it all comes down to energy. We are energy beings. We are made up of different types of energy: physical, mental, emotional, and spiritual. When our energy bodies (and our lives) are in balance, everything is in top working condition. When one or more of these areas become unbalanced, our body tries to heal itself. Our bodies are the healer, and up until a certain point, the body can heal everything. But the body needs enough energy—life force energy—to do that. Think of your life force energy as the gas tank of a car. When the gas runs out, the car no longer moves. When the body has exhausted its own energy, it cannot heal itself. A Reiki session will refill your body with life-force energy so that it can come back into balance.

Reiki energy works on all levels: physical, mental, emotional, and spiritual. It can help the body heal issues that correspond to all of those areas and even works across all areas that are involved. For example, there may be illness or disease in some part of the body, but it can come from many different causes: physical, mental, emotional, spiritual, and even a combination of those. Reiki will go to the root causes, shift/dissolve/clear those causes, and then fill that place in the energy bodies with higher-vibration energy.

I find that many of the root causes for clients come from past-life issues. The following is an experience I had with a first-time client on the day before she was to have major surgery.

After already having four major colon surgeries, including an emergency colostomy in just fourteen months, Kay's abdominal muscles had healed like a piece of Swiss cheese—filled with holes. Her colon had become trapped in one of the holes, and surgeons had planned a new, lengthy surgery for her: they would remove all of her abdominal muscles, rebuild them, and put them back in.

It was estimated that it would be a month before she could walk after that surgery and three months before she could walk normally.

The day before the surgery, Kay had her first Reiki session with me. Kay is an empath and intuitive and can feel and see things with her spiritual gifts. During her session, it felt to her like a hot geyser shot water from her root chakra to her heart chakra, and she kept hearing, "I'm alive...I'm alive...I'm alive." She also saw scenes in her mind of a Civil War soldier. In my own third eye, I could see an old-fashioned doctor's bag which looked like it had been through the entire war. I got an impression of a battleground with the dead and dying all around and could feel all the fear, anxiety, and dread of the situation.

The Reiki session lasted thirty minutes. Our intentions were past-life healing, healing for the root cause of what was going on in her abdomen, and also clearing of the cellular memory of what had happened to her body.

Her surgery was scheduled to last between six and eight hours. Instead, the doctors only needed two hours. They didn't need to take the muscles out and put them back in like they originally planned. Although the surgeons couldn't explain it, the muscles in Kay's abdominal walls had relaxed so much that they could perform hernia-like repairs. When Kay woke from that surgery, she could walk to her bed by herself.

As soon as she fully recovered, she became a student and learned Practical Reiki for herself.

Everyone can learn to work with Reiki. One doesn't need to be special or spiritual or gifted to access it. Reiki energy is available to everyone on this Earth plane. It is another tool in our toolbox that helps us to navigate our lives. But it is helpful to be guided by someone who has worked with it and can offer their experience and knowledge.

Will-IAM has said that working with energy is our Divine right. I feel like it is our responsibility as well. It is up to us to keep ourselves healthy physically, mentally, emotionally, and spiritually. If we look to others to do that for us, we are giving our power away. But most importantly, we are missing out on the huge spiritual growth that we can achieve when we actively participate in creating and clearing, shaping and changing our own lives.

One thing I hear the most from students is that they don't feel "qualified" to learn Reiki. Some feel like they are so wounded, their lives so dysfunctional, that they will fail. They feel like they need to be "perfect" before they can start that journey. It is exactly the opposite. If you have things in your life that you would like to change, Will-IAM invites you to step into your power and become your own soul alchemist. He'll guide you.

A big part of Reiki class is the energy attunements. These are very strong clearing sessions that remove blocks from the student so that he can access Reiki more deeply. These blocks can be on the physical, mental, emotional, or spiritual levels. Will-IAM says it is a ceremony that introduces you to the energy and the energy to you. Now that Will-IAM is completely embodied, he facilitates these attunements. That makes these sessions the purest, strongest, most high-vibrational connection possible.

Everything can be done over distance. There is no need to be in the same room for either a Reiki class or a Reiki session. Energy has no limitations. Just as you can listen to music without the orchestra being in your home, you can receive Reiki energy without being in the same room as the facilitator.

Please see my website for more information:

https://iamsoulalchemist.com/
learn-practical-reiki-become-your-own-soul-alchemist

Healing With Metatron

A few years after learning Practical Reiki, I added Metatronic Healing. This was something a friend had learned and was teaching, and I was immediately called to it. (I love working with Metatron, and he brought me Metatron's Astrology Cube many years later.)

This healing modality is very strong, and the teacher prepares you to receive this energy many days before the attunement. I remember one night waking up, and my eyes were still closed. My bedroom was filled with brilliant white light, which I could see through my third eye. There was a huge orb next to me. I had never seen an orb so large. It extended from floor to ceiling. I heard words that, to this day, I do not exactly remember. They either said, "We are preparing you," or "We are repairing you." But they both mean kind of the same thing.

I feel like the Metatronic energy integrated into the energy I was already using, so I didn't work with it exclusively. The energy I was channeling and using was becoming blended and alchemized. Shortly after being attuned to Metatron, I became attuned to Arcturian energy.

The Galactic Light Beings

A friend of a friend who was a brilliant psychic, medium, reader, and healer was teaching classes on the Ascended Galactic Light Beings—the Arcturians, Pleidians, and the Sirians. There was a small group of us that wanted to learn, so he came to my friend's home. There he spoke in the light language of each dimension. When I heard the language, I burst into tears and cried for a long time. I wasn't expecting it and didn't know why, but it felt like I was remembering something from a long, long time ago that I thought I would never hear again. I remembered how lonely I had always felt and how I felt like I never fit in on this planet. This was ancient grief.

The Ascended Masters at the Ascension portal through <alphaimaging.co.nz> offer an Ancient Grief healing session. I signed up for one of those, and after the session, Verna confirmed that I had had grief in every cell of my body, which had been cleared. That totally resonated with me.

A few days after this, I was shown a specific kind of Arcturian energy and how to work with it. This happened in a dream. It was so surreal. They were working on me, and yet I was also a spectator watching them do it. This is an energy that must be called in at the moment; it is not something that can be alchemized. Not long after this, I badly burned my finger on a hot pan. I immediately put Reiki on it, and it hardly made a dent in the pain. Something told me to ask for the Arcturian energy, and within a minute the pain was gone. Not only that, there was no evidence of a burn—no blister, no red mark, nothing. Like it had never happened. That was amazing!

I've always been a student, and I love to learn. I used to read every spare minute of every day when I was younger. I started to read more about different healing modalities and practiced with them. I had long recognized that my spirit guides and angels would bring me those things I needed to do and work with. (This was all before my Higher Self was even a gleam in my eye, so to speak.) I worked with Diamond Crystalline Light, Mahatma Energy, the Threefold Flame, and Christos Energy. I'm sure there are some that I'm forgetting. I also worked with the energy of crystals. Not so much with the crystals themselves (although I love them), but with their energy and vibration that can be channeled.

My Ascension Path

I was starting to dabble on the Ascension path, but that was slow going until I left the church. My son helped me with that. When he was five years old, he started to see and hear spirits. That was an entirely new learning curve for me. It was probably sometime in 2009 (of course!), as I was driving him to religion class, that he announced he didn't want to go there anymore because his guides told him that 90 percent (or more) of what was being taught was incorrect. My son has the ancient Egyptian gods as spirit guides, especially Anubis.

So I started the slow and arduous process of leaving the Catholic religion. I never left the faith, though. Mother Mary was my Ascension teacher and is still one of the Ascended Masters that I feel closest to, along with Jesus and Archangel Michael—after my Higher Self, of course. As a Catholic, I didn't know about St. Germain and Metatron, but those Masters would come later. I feel like I just let go of the rules and the limitations of the organized religion and kept all of the true essence: love, devotion, acceptance, and miracles. I feel closer to the Ascended Masters and my Higher Self than ever before because nothing stands in the way of our connection.

My Higher Self

Finally, it was 2018, and I had reached the fifth initiation. I will never forget it. My husband and I were taking my son to college for the first time. I could feel all the energetic shifts and changes in my light body system. It was exhausting, and I had never felt so tired, but it was exciting as well. My son and I were both starting new life journeys, but each in a different way.

Up until that point, I had been preparing myself to be able to work with my Higher Self, even though I didn't know it. I had worked out of two different metaphysical shops and my home for years doing the following: giving tarot and astrology readings, teaching Reiki and giving energy sessions, and participating in monthly Reiki shares. I was always working on clearing out my own blocks and issues, and constantly reading and learning new things about astrology. I just kept going, and I'm still going. There is always something new to learn, and my Higher Self is teaching me all the time. I am devoted to this work, and this work is all I do. It's not a job or calling; it's my life.

During a healing session, I was shown a purple graduation gown. That's how I knew that we (my Higher Self and I) were on the seventh ray. That is the ray of magic and mystery, transformation, transmutation, and alchemy. It's what I had been doing all along for years—taking the old and turning it into gold; taking the ego and turning it into soul.

My Higher Self's name is Will-IAM. One day he told me his name as we were going into a group meditation. His name is so appropriate—he helps people who have gotten lost to find themselves again. People who wonder about themselves, "Who am I?" are ready to hear from Will-IAM. He can reconnect them to their own personal *I AM*, whatever that may be.

I don't "see" my Higher Self as some initiates see theirs. I feel him. He has been in full embodiment for about two-and-a-half years as I am writing this. About a year ago, there was a significant shift in how I perceived him. At that time I had been feeling him outside of me. Then I started to fully surrender into being one with Will-IAM. I let go of trying to control things and having to worry about things and started just to trust and be. Now I feel as if I am inside Will-IAM.

We are together every day. I talk to him all the time. Sometimes a fun song will come on the radio, and I invite him to sing with me. (And sometimes I can really hear him!) Will-IAM is creative and loves to dance and sing and have fun. He is powerful, but accomplishes all with ease and grace, joy, and lightness of being. He teaches me that life doesn't have to be hard. Life is an adventure—an endless magic carpet ride where we can do anything and everything, and we are always experiencing something new. He has given me this catchphrase, "Live, live, live!" and it is a good reminder not to sweat the small stuff.

I.AM.Soul Astrology Readings

Our readings are unique because they are both readings and healings. A great deal of energy runs through the session. My voice changes, and when that happens there are light codes coming through that dissolve blockages, as seen and talked about in the birth chart. These codes are also like seeds that are planted—they continue to grow and keep working long after the session is over. It is like putting a little bit of magic into the birth chart. I will also cough out the really strong stuck energy. Will-IAM is constantly putting his ray energies and healing through the client as well, and that can become very strong at times. The clients receive what they are ready for and what is perfect for them.

Will-IAM tells me that our readings reflect the person's soul back to them. I look at a birth chart as a graphic representation of the Akashic records—the record of all of a soul's past lives. The blocks and the wounds can be seen there as well as the gifts and the talents.

It is hard to describe the healing that can come forward during this process. Everybody is different, and everybody's reading is different. But one thing that happens for everyone is that they are going to fall in love with their soul again, as I have. They are going to receive confirmation, epiphanies, enlightenment, and an explanation of what has been going on in their lives that take their consciousness up to a new level. Instead of, "This is what has been happening to me," they come away with, "This is what is happening for me," or "This is what my soul has been learning." They are going to be able to look at their life with new eyes—their soul's eyes. They're going to have some big *a-ha* moments when they realize their struggles, issues, and even suffering at times have a higher purpose. They receive a lot of clarity on what to do next.

One thing I hear the most from people is, "So I'm not crazy after all!" followed by, "I knew it!" or "I thought so/I hoped so." Suddenly everything makes sense; the gears all align and lock into place, and things start moving.

During an astrology reading, Will-IAM connects with the client on a quantum level. His energy is everywhere in the reading. His vibration comes through my voice the entire time, and his energy continually shines through the session—inspiring them, clearing them, motivating them. These sessions are over two hours long, and that is quite a long time to sit with an Ascended Master! Some clients have shared that they have taken naps after their readings, and everybody needs to get grounded and drink lots of water afterward.

Here is one client's experience with her I.AM.Soul astrology reading (the reading that I channel over distance, and we are not together):

> "I came to Tammy after my daughter, Hayden Jae, had been born 'still' a couple of months before. I was seeking a deeper meaning and a sense of purpose after my daughter's death. Being sensitive to energy, I knew that Tammy was working within my soul, but when my reading arrived in my inbox, I was absolutely blown away at the things that she said to me after knowing nothing about me, with the exception of my birth date, time, and where I was born. Within the first few minutes, the energy that her Higher Self brought to my soul reverberated through my body, and I found myself weeping as she spoke for the next couple of hours about things that I had felt my whole life, but I had never been able to identify or put into words.

> "She said things to me that only the shadow parts of myself had started even to scratch the surface of, but she said it with such conviction. It felt as though we had known each other for years, and she had walked a path with me that not many have. Her Higher Self delves into your soul and finds your life path and purpose while actively healing and clearing past life, trauma, blockages, and all of the things that are holding you back in the present day and this physical human experience. I can say that listening to my reading multiple times, I would hear new things, feel new things, and the point is that after I had my reading, I felt as though a door had been opened for me in a way that I hadn't seen before. All the healing energy, and her ability to touch my soul, helped me curate and allow myself to be open to new opportunities and possibilities in life after my daughter died."

Many clients have told me that when they listen to the recording again—in a week, in a month, in a year—they hear something that they had not previously heard. Something comes to their attention in a new way or in Divine timing. Possibly they weren't ready to hear it before, but now they are.

In a reading with another client, which was also channeled remotely, we each had the distinct impression that a barrier of some sort had been removed. We don't know what that was, but Will-IAM did. There will be many things that will be shifted and cleared during a reading that we won't be conscious of, but we can perceive changes going forward.

This client did notice that she felt happier and lighter afterwards, and her face even looked different, like it was smoother and clearer. She also had a major sinus problem from an infection many years ago. She felt like that had eased as well. She used to have difficulties sleeping and not remembering her dreams. After the reading, she noticed that she was sleeping better, dreaming every night, and remembering the dreams. The astrology reading will work on all levels: physical, mental, emotional, spiritual...and on past lives as well.

Will-IAM is of the seventh ray, the ray of change, transformation and transmutation, and magic. The people that come to sit with Will-IAM are either already in the midst of deep changes or will start shifting soon. Will-IAM has two sub-rays: yellow and green, and this energy will come through the reading as well. Yellow is the second ray, the ray of wisdom, lightness of being, and joy. The second ray is the happiness ray. Green is the fifth ray of healing, truth, and knowledge. This ray is about understanding themselves and the world they live in. Will-IAM brings all these aspects into the session.

I bring in my knowledge of astrology from many past lives—and there have been many, going all the way back to ancient Rome. In one of my lifetimes in ancient Rome, I was a woman astrologer who advised the emperor. I find that amazing considering how limited women's lives were in that era. I get a kick out of knowing that I was a rebel even then and living my passion, even if it was dangerous. And it was certainly dangerous to advise the emperor because your life was only as good as your last reading! Luckily the clients who come now are truly wonderful, and they have each touched my soul as I sit in their presence.

Metatron's Astrology Cube

Astrology charts are our Akashic records in symbolic form. All of our past lives are contained in that blueprint, and we can do more than just read the energy. We can heal what is there as well.

I have a friend who is a wonderful spiritual leader and healer with the gift of clairaudience (among many others). One day she messaged me and asked, "When was the last time you talked to Metatron? He wants to talk to you." Mind blown!

I sat with Metatron in a torus meditation, and I could feel all his energy and knowledge that he was downloading into me. In my third eye, I could see the image of an astrology chart and the sacred geometry of Metatron's cube. I started to experiment with this on myself and then with friends.

The energy that was being cleared from the chart was amazing—very deep, yet very fast. It clears multidimensionally from past lives. If this calls to you, please see my website for more details.

https://iamsoulalchemist.com/metatrons-astrology-cube

Relationship Chart Clearing

Will-IAM gave me this healing as I was outside meditating in the sun two summers ago. He reminded me that when we have a relationship with someone, that relationship also has an astrology chart which is something that can also be cleared. This relationship chart clearing can be done for you and your parents, your children, your spouse, and your friends. This clearing can also be done with someone with whom there is no longer a relationship, such as an ex-partner or ex-spouse. (Even with a person who has passed on into spirit.) It can clear out old baggage and bring you peace and closure.

This is what clients have to say about this session: "Life is starting to be less difficult."

From a client who had done this session with her husband: "My partner and I are communicating better—softer and less aggressively. I now have the courage to say what I think. Life is feeling pretty good since I have done this session, and for the first time in my life, I feel like I can relax and not watch my P's and Q's."

For more details, please see my website:

https://iamsoulalchemist.com/relationship-chart-clearing-session

Pattern Healing/Past-Life Healing

I am particularly fascinated with this aspect of healing. I believe, from my experience working with myself and with clients, that everything in our current life can be traced back to a point of origin—a past life. The circumstances may not be exactly the same, but the issues resonate. We can go back to the past life of origin and clear that issue and everything that was created because of it, through that life and all subsequent lives, and through the current lifetime. I have seen people's lives change that way. I've changed my own life that way.

Everything can change, from your relationship with yourself and with others to relationships with food, money—whatever you want to change. If you can identify it, you can change it. We also create new timelines of a higher vibration to take the place of the old issues that have been cleared.

Again, these sessions are difficult to describe because everybody is going to have a different experience. But I have found that we each have several past lifetimes that sit very "heavy" on us karmically in the current lifetime. I feel like it has something to do with the birth chart. Everything is numbered in the chart, and these are called "degrees." It seems to me that the soul can't advance to the next degree of the birth chart when there is major unfinished business or something huge that is "stuck" at a certain point—hence the lifetime that sits very heavy on us. It's like we are reliving it to get it right this time.

When we clear these, everything will change. I found a past lifetime like that for myself a few years ago. When I started to research this lifetime, I found that many people I knew from my current life were also with me in that past life. Even somebody that I knew for a semester in college had been an important part of that lifetime for me! I cleared and cleared this lifetime, and things got better, but something was still stuck. Finally, I found that I had made a promise to myself and to others—which is why things were not moving. When I rescinded all the promises, I was finally free.

The following is a recent experience with a client doing pattern clearing from past lives:

> "Tammy told me about her new clearing session. Her Higher Self always shows her new and neat healing techniques! I said I am absolutely up for it! When we began, I never knew what we would stumble on. Tammy starts the session by asking me what I need to clear and looks at some of the alignments in my astrology chart...we could see where some energy needed to shift. I said to Tammy, 'I am just so angry all the time, and it is worse at work!' This is the amazing part...as she asks some questions, we get to my inner child. All I kept seeing was myself, but a young version. She was blonde, just pure innocence with flowers on her hair. Just dancing around in a white dress. But I just knew this little girl was love. Tammy began to cry, which made me cry even more because she isn't usually so emotional! Tammy said that the lifetime felt angelic, and she kept seeing wings. In my clearing and in my life, I would get sharp piercing heart pains, and Tammy didn't know until I told her. It turned out that this lifetime we had found was a

> sainted lifetime where I devoted myself to Merciful Love and took on the pain of the world into my physical body. Which is absolutely what I have been doing for many years! Tammy and I both cried but were in utter awe!
>
> "This was just a true gift to have done because not only did it bring back gifts, it cleared huge blocks for me instantly that had not wanted to go. I had tried to clear them, but we finally found a specific life at the root of the problem and cleared a lot off. It is a relief to have it moved, but even more a gift to know we are soul sisters from that lifetime. Right away I felt the heart pain move. I am less angry and lighter. I do believe stuff is shifting, but I also recognize the patterns more clearly now."

I should say something about crying. Sometimes I do cry during a session, whether it be an astrology reading or an energy clearing. Sometimes I cry it out because the client is holding the emotion and they can't cry for themselves. Sometimes I cry because there is just so much emotion involved, and it's a way to release. Sometimes I cry just sitting with someone's soul because it's so beautiful and lovely, it touches my own soul. I never know when it will happen, but it's okay—I just keep a box of Kleenex in my healing room.

https://iamsoulalchemist.com/pattern-unraveling

There are many tools and techniques that Will-IAM has taught me. He gives me specific words or phrases and specific techniques. He is always teaching me something new. I always do what he shows me, and I never doubt it. I am always ready to do more and to learn more, and then he shows me the next thing. I love this life that we have together, and I am happy and excited every day to do this work. It is an honor and a privilege to hold this space for people to help them reconnect to their soul...to get their lives back...to find themselves again...to recreate themselves in a new version...to find joy or love or peace again...everything and anything is possible.

Tammy Manzo, USA

www.iamsoulalchemist.com

Appendix A

– List of Contact Information

Here is a convenient list of the website, social media, and contact information for each of the healers in this book. The website for Ascension information is also provided.

Chapter One: "Healing Art Heals the Soul" by Tamara Liz Rivera Hyde.

Email: becreative@tamaraliz.com.

Website: www.tamaraliz.com

Website: www.espiritucreativo.org

Facebook: Facebook.com/TamaraLiz

YouTube: @tamaraliz

Ascend: @5thraymaster

Instagram: @tamaraliz.art

TikTok: @tamaralizart

Chapter Two: "Energetic Blockages in the Chakras Affect Both Humans and Animals" by Hayatti Rahgeni.

Website: www.powercreatefreedom.com.

Be our Patron: www.patreon.com/hayattirahgeni

Subscribe to our YouTube: www.youtube.com/powercreatefreedom

Follow our Instagram: www.instagram.com/powercreatefreedom

Like our Facebook Page: www.facebook.com/powercreatefreedom

Chapter Three: "Embodying the Priestess: Turning Pain into Power" by Charlene Locke.

Charlene Locke, United Kingdom: and Luxor, Egypt: Retreats, Energy Alchemy and Group Sessions Worldwide

For information about retreats, email: charlene@trinityretreats.com or Phone: +44 738 715 9102

For general inquiries, email: info@charlenelocke.com

Instagram: charlenelocke_energyalchemy

Facebook: Charlene Locke Energy Alchemy

Chapter Four: "Your Home as Your Sanctuary" by Carol Anne Halstead

Website: www.ascensiondowsing.com

Facebook: https://www.facebook.com/ascensiondowsing

Chapter Five: "A Lotus in Troubled Soil: Reconnecting to Joy Within" by Joy Vottus.

Website & Blog: https://www.awakeningwithjoy.com/

Facebook Group: https://www.facebook.com/groups/awakeningwithjoy/

YouTube: https://youtube.com/c/AwakeningwithJoy

Instagram: https://www.instagram.com/joy333.awakening.ascend/

Chapter Six: "All Our Answers Lie Within - Healing Through Love and Forgiveness" by Jan Thompson

Website: www.ascensionarts.ca

Website: www.ascensiondowsing.com

Facebook: https://www.facebook.com/ascensiondowsing

Chapter Seven: "You've Got This" by Kimberley Roles

Website: https://kimberleekorner.com

YouTube: Kimberlee Korner

Instagram: @iamkjroles

Facebook: Kimberley Roles ~ Kimberlee Korner and Kids Yoga by Kim

Chapter Eight: "From Birth to Rebirth: How I Became a Healer" by Lori Diebold

Lori Diebold: The Healing Heart

Website: https://www.thehealingheart.love

Instagram: @thehealingheart.love

Chapter Nine: "From Chaos to Unconditional Love" by Heather Corinne Lang

Website: www.NamasteRays.com

Facebook: https://www.facebook.com/heather.lang.19

Instagram: https://www.instagram.com/heatherclang/

Chapter Ten: "Turning the Old into Gold" by Tammy Manzo

Website: www.iamsoulalchemist.com

https://iamsoulalchemist.com/relationship-chart-clearing-session

https://iamsoulalchemist.com/metatrons-astrology-cube

Other Websites of Interest:

Ascension with the Ascended Masters: Learn in accurate detail about the Ascension path followed by the healers in this book@

Website: www.alphaimaging.co.nz

The Ascending Initiates: Read in more detail about the healers in this book. Connect with them through their photo images@

Website: www.ascendinginitiates.com